# THE INDEPENDEN'

CW00498383

# WALT DISNEY WORLD 2021

**G. Costa**

**Limit of Liability and Disclaimer of Warranty:**
The publisher has used its best efforts in preparing this book, and the information provided herein is provided "as is." Independent Guides and the author make no representation or warranties with respect to the accuracy or completeness of the contents of this book and specifically disclaim any implied warranties of merchantability or fitness for any particular purpose and shall in no event be liable for any loss of profit or any other commercial damage, including but not limited to special, incidental, consequential, or other damages.
Please read all signs and safety information before entering attractions, as well as the terms and conditions of any third party companies used. Prices are approximate, and do fluctuate.

**Contact us:**
If you have questions about this book or the resort, get in touch via our website at www.independentguidebooks.com - we are happy to help.

# Contents

**An Important Message Regarding the Pandemic:**

At the time we were writing and updating this guide, the world was undergoing a global pandemic, Covid-19. We have included the latest information as to how this may affect your visit. Although most of the changes that are going to be made have already happened by now, there may be additional changes in 2021, especially as things return to normal. We also include how things work in 'regular times' as we expect most of these procedures to return in 2021.

Your visits may be affected by enhanced crowd control and social distancing measures and the possible cancellation (or changes) to shows, attractions, dining experiences, transportation, and meet-and-greets. Check the official website at www.disneyworld.com for any changes that may affect your vacation. Look out for the virus symbol throughout the guide for specific changes.

# Introduction

Walt Disney opened Disneyland in California in 1955 – here Disney fans could meet their favorite characters, families enjoyed time together, and dreams came true every day.

The park was a great success, but as Disneyland was built in a residential area, other hotels and shops started to surround the park with guests seeing billboards towering from inside the park and the illusion of an imaginary world was easily broken.

In the 1960s, Walt Disney developed his "Florida Project", a hugely expanded version of Disneyland. Disney began to secretly buy up part of central Florida bit by bit – 47 square miles of it; this was the beginning of "Disney World".

Sadly, in 1966, Walt Disney passed away and the plans for Disney World almost collapsed. Despite the loss of its founder, the company built Walt's dream, and in 1971 Magic Kingdom Park was unveiled. This park was based on Disneyland, but on a grander scale.

In 1982, EPCOT became the second theme park. It is a place to learn about the future, and to visit pavilions representing countries from around the world.

In 1989, Disney's Hollywood Studios became the third theme park – here guests can experience rides and shows inspired by movies.

Finally, in 1998 the fourth theme park opened - Disney's Animal Kingdom Park - where guests can learn about animals, venture on a safari and go on wild rides.

As well as theme parks, Walt Disney World contains two water parks, golf and mini-golf courses, 30 Disney resort hotels, horse-riding areas, backstage tours, spas, shopping and entertainment districts and much more. It really is a Disney world.

2021 is an extremely exciting year as the resort celebrates its 50th Anniversary!

## ACRONYMS IN THIS BOOK

**Animatronic** – The robots you will see in the rides and shows throughout the park.
**Attraction** – The general term for a ride, character meet, or show at the theme parks.
**Cast Member (CM)** – A Disney employee.
**Disney Resort** – A Disney hotel. Called resorts because of their theming and amenities.
**Disney Springs** – The shopping district of Walt Disney World Resort.
**FastPass+ (FP+)** – A free service to save you time waiting in line.
**Guest** – You, the person entering the theme park – you are not a mere visitor, but a guest!
**Off-Property** – Everything outside of Walt Disney World Resort's land.
**On-Property** – Everything that is within Walt Disney World Resort's 47 square miles of land.
**Standby Line** – The regular queue line for attractions for guests without a FastPass+ booking.
**Transportation and Ticket Centre (TTC)** – An area next to the Magic Kingdom Park's car parking lot. When arriving by car, you must go through the TTC to get a monorail or boat to Magic Kingdom Park. A monorail service also runs from the TTC to EPCOT.

# Getting There

## Flying

### Orlando International Airport (MCO) is our recommended airport – it is less than 25 miles from Walt Disney World.

• **Rental cars** – Most major car rental companies are on the Ground Transportation Level (Level 1).
•**Driving directions** – At the airport, follow Jeff Fuqua Blvd towards FL-417 S (a toll road - about $2.50). Follow signs to I-4/Tampa/Disney World. About 10.6 miles later, take Exit 6 for International Drive. Drive onto FL-536 W / World Center Drive. Follow signs towards your hotel from here. The total distance is about 20-25 miles and 25-40 minutes.
•**Shuttles** – These small buses generally cost $25 per person one-way to locations on Disney World property. These are shared with others. Return trips are $40 per person.
•**Taxis and Uber** – Cheaper than shuttles for large groups (up to 9 people) and you get a private vehicle. Taxis are metered and

should cost about $65 to $90 one-way to Walt Disney World. An Uber is about $35-$40 one-way.
•**Disney Magical Express** – A complimentary return service to Disney's hotels. Available for both domestic and international guests. On return, guests can check-in for their flight (selected airlines only) at their hotel.

### Orlando Sanford Airport (SFB) – 43 miles from Walt Disney World.

• **Rental Cars** – Several companies have offices on airport property.
•**Driving directions** (tolls apply): Join and follow FL-417 North for approximately 3.3 miles, take the I-4 West towards Kissimmee. After 39.5 miles on the I-4, you will be in the Walt Disney World area. Follow local Disney signs. Total drive: 43 miles, and 45-50 minutes.
•**Shuttles** – Orlando Carriers, Inc. (407-418-0513) provides a shuttle service. Orlandoshuttleservice.com allows you to compare and

book providers online. We have not used either service. About $50 per person each way for a shuttle.
•**Taxis and Uber** – About $130 to $170 each way from the airport to Walt Disney World. There are often discounts for booking a round-trip fare. Mearstransportation.com is the recommended company at the airport. An Uber is $60 to $80.

### Miami International Airport (MIA) – If you are flying into here be prepared for a long transfer time as the airport is about 230 miles away from Walt Disney World (3.5 hours of driving). Unless you get an incredible deal on flights, airfare savings are soon eliminated by the cost of transfers and lost time.

•**An Internal Flight** – Catch a 1-hour internal flight from Miami International Airport (MIA) to Orlando (MCO).
•**Rental Car** – At the Rental Car Centre. Several rental car companies operate.

## Rail

Although cross-country public transport is far from world-class in the US, you can travel from most cities in the North East to Orlando, Florida by Amtrak trains in 18 to 24 hours.

This can be a less stressful way of traveling than flying or driving but is also slower. Dining coaches are available on long-distance Amtrak

trains.

Cross-country trips are more complicated. Visit amtrak.com for details. From Orlando's Amtrak station you will need a taxi or Uber to Disney World.

Example pricing scenario: A round-trip journey from New York Penn Station to Orlando, Florida booked 10

weeks in advance for February 2021 costs $77 for a saver seat, $154 for one adult in a "value" coach seat. A flexible fare is around $335.

The same journey in a "roomette" with some meals included and a bed costs $481 for one person or $682 for two sharing.

# Hotels

*Having a place to relax after a long day in the parks is essential during a Walt Disney World Resort visit. Thankfully, there are many accommodation options including official Disney-operated hotels and even villas. These serve a wide range of budgets and are located right in the heart of the magic.*

There are also partner hotels located on Walt Disney World Resort property, but not run by Disney itself. Plus, there are hundreds of nearby hotels off-property. Central Florida is a hugely competitive market meaning some world-class luxury hotels are available, as well as many mid-range and budget options.

The on-site hotels are split into four categories:

- **Value** - All Star Resorts (Music, Movies, and Sport), Art of Animation, Pop Century and The Campsites at Fort Wilderness Resort
- **Moderate** - Caribbean Beach, Port Orleans (French Quarter and Riverside), Coronado Springs and The Cabins at Fort Wilderness Resort
- **Deluxe** - Animal Kingdom Lodge, Beach Club, BoardWalk Inn, Contemporary Resort, Grand Floridian Resort & Spa, Polynesian Village Resort, Wilderness Lodge, and Yacht Club.
- **Deluxe Villa** - Bay Lake Tower at Disney's Contemporary Resort, Boulder Ridge Villas at Wilderness Lodge, Animal Kingdom Villas (Jambo House and Kidani Village), Beach Club Villas, BoardWalk Villas, Old Key West Resort, Polynesian Villas & Bungalows,  Saratoga Springs Resort & Spa, Disney's Riviera Resort, and The Villas at Disney's Grand Floridian Resort & Spa.

Generally speaking, the more expensive hotels have more elaborate theming, more A We highly recommend an on-site hotel for a Walt Disney World stay if you can justify the cost. Over the next few pages, you will discover all the extra advantages of staying on-site.

☼ **COVID-19 CHANGES:**
As of December 2020, all Disney's hotels are open (except All Star Resorts with a target date of Feb 9, 2021 and Polynesian Village Resort with a target date of Summer 2021). Disney's Beach Club Resort and Disney's BoardWalk Inn do not currently have a reopening date. Character dining and dinner shows are not operating at any on-site hotel. Club level rooms and lounges are unavailable. The Extra Magic Hours benefit is unavailable. Guest rooms receive a light cleaning every other day, with a full clean between guests. Online check in is recommended, although not compulsory. In-room dining is unavailable. The resort airline check-in service is unavailable. Some dining locations are closed at resorts.

Face coverings are required for guests ages 2 and up at all times at the resort hotels except inside guest rooms, when by the pool, swimming, or eating while stationary. Guests will be temperature screened.

# Disney Resort Hotels

*The Walt Disney World Resort offers thirty Disney owned resorts on property, covering all price ranges, including Value, Moderate and Deluxe rooms, as well as Deluxe Villas. All are beautifully themed environments and offer distinct advantages over other non-Disney hotels.*

## Disney Hotel Features and Amenities

- **Optional MagicBands** with your room key, park tickets, meal vouchers, PhotoPass and more on a wearable bracelet (small charge).
- **Laundry facilities** for $3 per load; dryers: $3 a load. Detergent: $1 per load.
- **In-room babysitting services** are available from $18 per hour at all resorts. The Dolphin Resort and Contemporary Resort also offer paid Children's Activity Centers and activities.
- **Entertainment** at your hotel - all hotels have an arcade and host outdoor nightly Disney movie screenings. Other activities may include basketball, bike and boat rentals, carriage rides, golf courses, archery, fishing, golf cart rentals, jogging paths, gyms, pony rides, tennis courts, and volleyball courts.
- **Late checkout** (subject to availability) at no extra cost.

- **Local calls** are 75 cents; there is no charge for calls within Walt Disney World.
- **No charge for children under 17** staying in the same room as adults. In rooms with more than two adults, extra adults pay a supplement of $15 to $35 each per night.
- **A Disney shop** in each resort selling merchandise and basic sundry items.
- **Room occupancy** at Disney hotels is usually 4 people.
- **A 24-hour front desk**.
- **Overnight self-parking** costs $13 at Value resorts, $19 at Moderates, and $24 at Deluxes, per night.
- **Room service** in all rooms for a $3 delivery fee plus 18% gratuity.
- **At least one ATM** per resort.
- **Check-in** is at 3:00pm and check out is at 11:00am for all resorts unless stated.
- **All Disney resorts are non-**smoking except in designated areas.
- **Room amenities** include cable TV, coffee-making facilities, a telephone, a table with two chairs, and an in-room safe. Most standard rooms have 2 double beds or 1 king-size.
- **Special rates** for annual passholders, guests with a Disney Visa card and Florida Residents - up to 40% off.
- **Room prices** vary seasonally. Prices listed herein are per night for a standard room with two adults sharing, and include tax at 12.5% (unless stated), and exclude special offers.

## EXCLUSIVE DISNEY HOTEL ADVANTAGES

- **Complimentary transportation** to all the theme parks, using buses, monorails and boats.
- **Extra Magic Hours**, allowing one hour's early entry into one theme park per day, and to stay up to two hours after park closing at another park. (Suspended due to COVID-19)
- **Free parking** at the theme parks and water parks with your MagicBand.
- **Free round-trip Magical Express transportation** to and from Orlando International Airport.
- **Complimentary in-room Wi-Fi** and at most public areas at resorts.
- **At least one pool per hotel.**
- **Disney Dining Plans** available with package bookings – savings of up to 40% on meals (suspended due to COVID-19). Where you see DDP in restaurant listings this means that that dining location typically accept the Disney Dining Plan.
- **A small refrigerator** in every room.
- **A refillable mug program** ($20) with unlimited drink refills at resort hotels for your stay.
- **Resort Airline Check-In** (suspended due to COVID-19) – Check in for flights directly from your resort, including checking in luggage and receive a boarding card. Available for both domestic and international passengers flying with: Alaska, American, Delta (domestic only), JetBlue, Southwest, and United.

# All Star Resorts

This 5840-room Value resort is actually three separate hotels next to each other. Each has giant sculptures and characters appropriate to the theme. All-Star Resorts are the cheapest in all of Walt Disney World, so you may find that the hotel is booked by large groups such as cheerleading teams.

There are no Table Service restaurants at these hotels - only food-court options.

Theming at these hotels is suited for younger members of the family who will likely enjoy seeing big Disney character icons around the resort. The theming will not, however, transport you to a different place in the way that some of the more premium resorts do.

Overall, these resorts offer a great value stay for guests

on a limited budget and who spend most of their time in the parks.

**All-Star Movies** - Five movie-themed buildings including one themed to 101 Dalmatians and another to Toy Story. Rooms have movie-themed touches. There are two pools. This is the best themed of the three All-Star resorts, we think.

**All-Star Sports** - There are three pools. McDonald's is a 5-minute walk from the resort entrance.

**All-Star Music** – As well as standard rooms, there are family suites of 520ft$^2$ for up to 6 people. There are two bedrooms  bathrooms in suites, two TVs, a pullout sofa, a microwave and fridge.

**Location**: Animal Kingdom resort area.
**Theme**: Movies, Music & Sports.
**Transport**: Buses to all Walt Disney World locations – 10 to 15 minutes to Animal Kingdom Park, EPCOT and Disney's Hollywood Studios, and 20 minutes to the water parks and Magic Kingdom.
**Room size**: 260 ft$^2$.
**Room prices**: $118-$254 for a standard room, $300-$581 at All Star Music family suites
**Activities**: Poolside movies and activities, and an arcade at each of the three resorts.

---

### DINING

**End Zone (Sports)** – Quick Service, DDP, entrées are $10-$14.50. Whole large pizzas $30.
**Grandstand Spirits (Sports)** – Pool Bar, No DDP. Drinks are $8-$15.
**Intermission Food Court (Music)** – Quick Service, DDP, entrées are $10-$14.50.
**Singing Spirits (Music)** – Pool Bar, No DDP. Drinks are $8-$15.
**World Premiere Food Court (Movies)** – Quick Service, DDP, entrées: $10-$14.50.
**Silver Screen Spirits (Movies)** – Pool Bar, No DDP. Drinks are $8-$15.

---

# Pop Century Resort

A step up from the All Star Resorts, Pop Century provides many of the same amenities as the other value resorts.

However, Pop Century Resort opened its doors in late 2003, making it newer than the All Stars (which opened in the 1990s), but older than Art of Animation Resort.

Given the slight increase in price we think this is worth the few extra dollars.

As well as the Everything Pop food court at this resort,  guests are a short walk away from Disney's Art of Animation Resort which has an even greater variety of food options.

This resort now also has

access to the convenient Disney Skyliner cable-car system with connections to EPCOT and Disney's Hollywood Studios. Buses are available to all other locations.

**Location**: Near ESPN Wide World of Sports; connected to Art of Animation resort.
**Theme**: Pop culture in the second half of the 20th

century. Expect to see giant play-doh sets, Disney characters, bowling pins, keyboards, 8 track tapes and much more.
**Transport**: Skyliner to Hollywood Studios (15 mins) and EPCOT (20 mins). Buses to all other locations.
**Room size**: 260 ft$^2$.
**Room prices**: $162 to $330 for a standard room
**Activities**: There are three pools, a playground, an arcade and a "pop jet playground" where jets of water shoot out of the ground.
**Extras**: There is a 5000-square foot store in the resort.

## DINING

**Everything Pop** – Quick Service and Snacks, DDP, entrées are $10.50-$15.
**Petals** – Pool Bar serving alcoholic and non-alcoholic drinks, No DDP, drinks are $5-$15.

# Art of Animation

Art of Animation is the gold standard for the Value resorts.

The theming and atmosphere at Art of Animation is vastly superior to the other Value resorts and is among some of the best on property; the food court is also one of the best on all of Disney property as it features a wide variety of choices.

Rooms at this resort are more expensive than both All Star and Pop Century Resorts, and the majority of rooms here are actually family suites.

Standard rooms at this resort are very popular and it is worth booking far in advance to secure them, as suites are significantly more expensive.

**Location**: Near ESPN Wide World of Sports, connected to Pop Century resort.
**Theme**: Split into four sections themed around Disney and Pixar classics. The Little Mermaid area offers standard rooms. Suites are available in the areas themed to Finding Nemo, Cars and The Lion King.
**Transport**: Skyliner to Hollywood Studios (15 mins) and EPCOT (20 mins). Buses to all other locations.
**Number of rooms**: 864 standard rooms, 1120 family suites.
**Room size**: 260 ft$^2$ in a standard room and 565 ft$^2$

in a suite.
**Room prices**: Standard rooms are priced between $188 and $353; suites are priced between $467 and $826.
**Activities**: Poolside activities, underwater speakers in the main pool, and an arcade.
**Extras**: The suites feature kitchenettes with a table, a master bedroom, and three different sleeping spaces.

## DINING

**Landscape of Flavors Food Court** – Quick Service and Snacks, DDP, entrées are $10-$15.

# Port Orleans

Port Orleans is split into two resorts - Riverside (2048 rooms) and French Quarter (1000 rooms). This is a moderate resort with larger rooms than Value resorts.

Port Orleans is our favorite moderate resort: it has fantastic immersive theming, and plenty of amenities - guests can use the amenities of both Riverside and French Quarter resorts.

The centerpiece of this resort is the Sassagoula River that flows towards the Disney Springs area.

The resort is also just a short boat ride away from the dining and shopping options at Disney Springs.

**Location**: Disney Springs resort area.
**Transport**: Buses to all locations; boats to Disney Springs.
**Room size**: 314 ft$^2$ for standard rooms.
**Room prices**: $256 to $434 for a standard room.
**Riverside Activities**: Five pools, a spa and a kids' pool. There is also an evening carriage ride available. Catch-and-release pole fishing activities are also available for $6 for 30 minutes. There is also a 2-hour fishing excursion priced $235 to $270 for 5 people.
**French Quarter Activities**: A dragon water slide, a games room, and a water playground by the pool. The pool is heated and has a Jacuzzi. Bike rentals are available.
**Extras**: Some rooms also contain a trundle bed.

## DINING

**Mardi Grogs (French Quarter)** – Pool Bar, No DDP, drinks are $4.50-$19.
**Scat Cat's Club (French Quarter)** – Drinks lounge, No DDP. Appetizers are $11-$14.
**Sassagoula Floatworks and Food Factory (French Quarter)** – Snacks and Quick Service, DDP, entrées are $6-$19. Large pizzas are $30.
**Boatwright's Dining Hall (Riverside)**– Table Service, DDP, entrées are $19-$36.
**Muddy Rivers (Riverside)** – Pool Bar, No Disney Dining Plan, drinks are $5.50-$19.
**River Roost (Riverside)** – Drinks lounge, No Disney Dining Plan. Appetizers are $7-$14.
**Riverside Mill** – Snacks & Quick Service, DDP, entrées are $9-$18. Large pizzas are $30.

# Coronado Springs

This 1967-room moderate resort is themed to the Southwest of the US with Mexican influences. This large resort is popular with convention attendees.

Coronado Springs is a large resort and the only moderate-level resort to include a fitness center.

The centerpiece of the resort is a lake, surrounded by beaches with hammocks. The pool here is also our favorite moderate-level one.

The resort is spread out meaning that it can take a while from your room to a food location or the hotel reception.

The resort has a separate category of rooms called the Gran Destino Tower.

**Location**: Animal Kingdom resort area.
**Transport**: Buses to all Walt Disney World locations. Disney's Hollywood Studios, Animal Kingdom Park and EPCOT are a 10-minute bus ride, and Blizzard Beach is just 5 minutes away. The furthest park is Magic Kingdom which is 20 minutes away by bus.
**Room size**: Standard room - 314 ft$^2$, Standard tower room 375 ft$^2$.
**Room prices**: Between $232 and $400 per night for a standard room. Gran Destino Tower standard rooms are $280 to $532.
**Activities**: Towering above the main pool is a Mayan pyramid and water slide, with an archaeological site

for the kids too. Surrey bike rentals are available. Every Wednesday, there is a *Viva Coronado Springs Fiesta* where guests can taste Mexican treats and take part in special recreational activities.

**Extras**: There is an air-conditioned 400-seat open-air-style market food court. There are 3 other restaurants and room service. There are arcades, bars, playgrounds and pools. The rooms are located in three villages around "Lago Dorado". This resort contains a convention center.

## DINING

**Maya Grill** – Table Service, DDP, entrées are $18-$62.
**El Merado de Coronado** – Quick Service, DDP, entrées are $8.50-$12.50.
**Rix Café** – Quick Service, DDP, entrées are $10-$12.50, pastries are $4.50-$5.50.
**Rix Sports Bar and Grill** – Drinks Lounge and Meals, DDP, entrées are $11 to $19.
**Siestas Cantina** – Quick Service and Bar, DDP, entrées are $12 to $17.
**The Laguna Bar** – Bar, DDP, drinks are $9.25-$12.50.
**Three Bridges Bar and Grill** - Casual Dining and Lounge, DDP, entrees are $12-$25.
**Dahlia Lounge** - Drinks Lounge, DDP, Tapas are $9 to $35, specialty wines are $69-$170
**Toledo** - Table Service, DDP, tapas are $10-$18, entrees are $30-$45, signature set menu - $129 for 2 people
**Barcelona Lounge** - Coffee and Drinks Lounge, DPP, coffees are $3.50-$10

# Caribbean Beach Resort

This is one of the most relaxing resorts in our opinion and also one of the largest. There is a 45-acre lake in the middle of the resort with paths leading to each building.

This resort is quite big and it can be a 15-minute walk or longer from Centertown (the hub of the resort with dining locations) to your room. This is great for a peaceful ambiance but can be annoying at the end of a long day in the parks. You may wish to consider an upgraded room closer to the resort hub. This is the only moderate resort to offer an option of rooms which sleep five people.

**Location**: Near EPCOT, Disney's Hollywood Studios and the Disney Springs area.
**Transport**: Skyliner to Hollywood Studios (5 mins) and EPCOT (15 mins). Buses to all other locations.
**Number of rooms**: 2112 rooms in 33 buildings, grouped into 6 villages.
**Room size**: 340 ft².
**Room prices**: $240 to $432 per night for a standard room. Pirate themed rooms cost $315 to $461 per night.
**Activities**: The Centertown area has food courts, restaurants, shops, arcades, pools, and a water slide. There are bike and boat

rentals too. There are four pools at this resort. Hammocks are available at no charge by the lake.
**Extras**: Pirate themed rooms are available at a surcharge. A two-hour Caribbean Pirate Adventure Cruise is available for kids ages 4-12 for $39 to $49.

## DINING

**Banana Cabana** – Pool Bar, No DDP.
**Centertown Market** – Quick Service, DDP, entrées are $9-$11.
**Sebastian's Bistro** – Table Service, DDP, entrées are $22-$34.
**Spyglass Grill** – Quick Service, DDP, entrées are $8-$14.50.

# Riviera Resort

Located in the EPCOT resort area, this Deluxe Villa resort offers 489 rooms.

Discover Europe and the Mediterranean as Walt Disney did at this new resort - that's Disney's storyline. We don't feel there is very much of a European vibe here, personally.

As well as a fantastic rooftop restaurant, there are beautiful gardens, fountains two pools (including a quiet pool), and a gym.

The resort offers studio, 1-2- and-3-bedroom villas, but also a unique smaller 2-person 'Tower Studio' with many features such as the bed, microwave, and a fridge built into the wall.

**Transport**: Skyliner to Hollywood Studios (5-10 mins) and EPCOT (15 mins). Buses elsewhere.
**Room Prices**: Tower Studios are $429 to $738. Deluxe Studios are $642 to $1025. A 1-bedroom villa is $911 to $1415, a 2-bed is $1443 to $2214 and a 3-bed is $2892

to $4677.
**Activities**: A gym, giant chess set, two pools - one with a water slide, water play area, fire pit, character breakfast and signature dining, and a chocolate workshop ($60).

## DINING

**Bar Riva** – Bar and Light Food, DDP, sandwiches are $12.50, salads are $10-$14, alcohol $7.50-$15.
**Topolino's Terrace - Flavors of the Riviera** – Signature Dining, DDP [2 credits at dinner], entrees: $30-$50 at dinner, breakfast character prix fixe menu is $42 for adult & $25 for kids
**Le Petit Café** – Quick Service, DDP on drinks, bakery items are $3.50-$7, coffees are $3-$5
**Primo Piatto** – Quick Service, DDP, pizzas are $12, salads are $10-$14, other entrees $13-$16

# Yacht Club Resort

The Yacht Club is a 630-room deluxe resort located next to EPCOT's World Showcase entrance on Crescent Lake. The Yacht Club is one of our favorite resorts on all of Walt Disney World property.

The resort's location is within walking distance of EPCOT, and a boat ride away from Disney's Hollywood Studios.

The 3.5-million liter pool is by far the best at Walt Disney World and is shared with the Beach Club Resort - the pool even has a sand bottom.

The Yacht Club feels like true a deluxe resort throughout and comes highly recommended.

**Transport**: EPCOT is a 5-minute walk, or you can catch the boat from the dock at the back of the hotel. Hollywood Studios is a 20-minute boat ride or a similar walk. You can reach Magic Kingdom Park, Animal Kingdom, the Disney water parks and Disney Springs by bus.
**Room size**: 380 ft$^2$
**Room prices**: Standard rooms cost between $504 and $883 per night.
**Activities**: The best pool at

Walt Disney World, with water jets, a water slide, a hot tub and a quiet pool. Fantasia Gardens mini-golf is located close by. There is also a volleyball court, a health club, jogging paths and an arcade.
**Extras**: This hotel also features a clothes store and an in-house barber.

## DINING

**Ale and Compass** – Table Service, DDP, entrées are $17-$34.
**Ale and Compass Lounge** – Lounge, serves Breakfast, DDP, appetizers are $9-$18, cocktails are $13-$15, beers are $6-$11, also serves wine.
**Beaches and Cream** – Table Service, DDP, entrées are $13-$17. Desserts and sundaes are the specialties here including the famous $35 'kitchen sink' which serves 4 people.
**Crew's Cup Lounge** – Drinks Lounge, No DDP. Bourbon is $15-$17, beers $6-$12, also wine.
**Hurricane Hanna's Grille** – Bar and Quick Service, DDP, entrées are $10-$12.
**Yachtsman Steakhouse** – Signature Table Service Restaurant, DDP (2 credits per person), entrées are $38-$135.

# Beach Club Resort

Located next to the Yacht Club, the Beach Club is a 585-room resort by EPCOT's World Showcase entrance.

The Beach Club is the sister resort of the Yacht Club and comes equally highly recommended with its amazing pool, beach-side charm, and great location.

For larger groups, the Beach Club Villas are also available comprising of studios, 1-bed, 2-bed and 3-bed apartments, and villas.

Overall, this resort feels slightly less busy that the Yacht Club next door, with fewer non-resident visitors.

**Transport**: EPCOT is a 5-minute walk, or you can catch the boat from the dock at the back of the hotel. Hollywood Studios is a 20-minute boat ride or a 20-minute walk. You can reach Magic Kingdom Park, Animal Kingdom Park, the Disney water parks and Disney Springs by bus.
**Room size**: 380 ft$^2$.
**Room prices**: Standard rooms are priced between $504 and $883 per night. 1 bedroom villas cost $765 to $1268 per night, and 3-bedroom villas are $2538 to $4232 per night.
**Activities**: The hotel has the best pool at Walt Disney World, with water jets, a water slide, a hot tub and a quiet pool. Fantasia Gardens mini-golf is located close by. There is a volleyball court, a health club, a jogging track,

an arcade, and tennis courts. There is a scavenger hunt available from Guest Services.
**Extras**: At Atlantic Wear and Wardrobe Emporium, you can buy swimwear and clothes, food, souvenirs and does film processing. Periwig's does haircuts. There are penny and quarter press machines and an ATM machine.

## DINING

**Cape May Café** – Character Buffet at Breakfast and Non-Character Buffet at Dinner, DDP, $42 per adult and $27 per child at breakfast, $55 per adult and $33 per child at dinner.
**Martha's Vineyard Lounge** – Drinks Lounge, No DDP. Serves appetizers priced between $9 and $14, plus a wide variety of drinks.

# Boardwalk Inn Resort

This small 378-room resort is themed to a seaside town's boardwalk. The Boardwalk is an attraction unto itself and is amazingly well-located by EPCOT.

The Boardwalk Inn is a fun resort with a unique 1920s and 1930s seaside charm theme. As with the two previous resorts, The Boardwalk is located just steps from EPCOT.

The Boardwalk Inn is one of Walt Disney World's more intimate resorts due to its small size. As well as standard rooms, there are studios, 1-bedroom and 2-bedroom apartments.

**Location**: Between EPCOT and Hollywood Studios.
**Transport**: A 5-minute walk to EPCOT, although a boat service is also available. Hollywood Studios is a 20-minute walk, or a boat takes the same time. Bus transportation to the rest of Walt Disney World.
**Room size**: 390 ft$^2$.
**Room prices**: $555 to $943 per night for a standard room. 1-Bedroom Boardwalk Villas are $765 to

$1268 per night, whereas the 3-Bedroom Grand Villas are $2538-$4232 per night.
**Activities**: A main pool with swimming tubes as well as two other pools, a health club and a private spa. Bike rentals are $7 per hour.

## DINING

**AbracadaBar** – Lounge, No DDP. Cocktails $13-$15, wines $12-$22 per glass, beers: $8-$9
**Big River Grille and Brewing Works** – Table Service, DDP, entrées are $12-$27.
**Boardwalk Bakery** – Snacks and Quick Service, DDP. Bakery items are $3-$5.
**Boardwalk Pizza Window** – Quick Service, DDP, pizza slices: $6-$7, whole pizzas: $21-$23.
**Boardwalk To Go** – Snacks, No DDP, entrées are $5-$15.
**ESPN Club** – Table Service, DDP, entrées are $15-$28.
**Flying Fish** – Signature Restaurant, DDP (2 Table Service credits), entrées are $33 to $59.
**Leaping Horse Libations** – Quick Service and Bar, DDP, entrées are $8-$12.
**Trattoria al Forno** – Table Service, DDP, entrées are $19-$39.

# Wilderness Lodge Resort

This 728-room deluxe hotel is a short boat journey away from Magic Kingdom Park. It immerses you into a turn-of-the-century National Park lodge.

Wilderness Lodge is one of our favorite themed resorts, as it feels like home from the moment you step inside. The woodland-style setting is the perfect invitation to relax.

**Transport**: Buses to all parks; there is also a boat service to Magic Kingdom Park and to Fort Wilderness resort.
**Room size**: 340 ft$^2$.
**Room prices**: Standard rooms are priced between $424 and $826 per night. Deluxe villas are also available with 1-Bedrooms priced between $731 and $1108 per night, and 2-Bedrooms between $1213 and $2196 per night. Studio villas are also available.
**Activities**: There are several pools, a water slide, two hot tubs, jogging paths, an arcade, boat and bike rentals, flag family, Wonders of The Lodge guided tours and a Hidden Mickey hunt.

**Extras**: Concierge rooms are available. Studios, 1-bedroom and 2-bedroom apartments are also available including the Copper Creek Villas.

# Animal Kingdom Lodge Resort

This 1293-room African-themed resort extends the magic of Disney's Animal Kingdom Park with animals roaming the savanna just outside your window.

Animal Kingdom Lodge Resort is a magical place to stay and is the closest thing you will get to experiencing a night in Africa while in Florida.

The resort features three different savannas, each with unique animals and a distinct look and feel.

Although all rooms have balconies at this resort, it should be noted that this does not mean they all have views of the savannas and animals - those views cost at least $170 more than standard rooms.

You are welcome to explore all the savannas during your stay. A guide detailing where to find different species is available in all guest rooms.

Many guests worry that the smells from the animals will reach the rooms, but this is not the case. Rooms are also soundproofed to keep out the animal noise.

**Transport**: Buses to all locations. An internal shuttle service operates.
**Room size**: 344 ft$^2$.

**Room prices**: $434 to $759 per night in a standard room. Jambo House and Kidani Village villas are priced at $674 to $1386 each night for a 1-bedroom, and $1076 to $2166 for a 2-bedroom.
**Activities**: There are many pools and a fitness center.
**Extras**: There are savannah safari options for an extra charge.

# Grand Floridian Resort & Spa

The Victorian-themed Grand Floridian is unmatched in splendor. This 900-room deluxe hotel's grounds are romantic, yet relaxed.

The hotel is a little more "stuffy" (but not snobby) and less fun than some of the other resorts, in our opinion. If you like "being waited on hand and foot", there is no better choice. Standard rooms are among the largest at the Walt Disney World resort, measuring 440 ft$^2$.

Most rooms at the resort are not in the main building and require a walk outdoors without shelter. This is something to bear in mind in case of inclement weather. These outer buildings are very peaceful.

Magic Kingdom Park is only a short monorail or boat ride away or a 12-minute walk, and there are fantastic views of Cinderella Castle from across the resort.

The on-site "Senses" spa offers facials, massages, body therapies, nails, kids services, and full spa packages.

**Location**: One stop from Magic Kingdom Park.
**Transport**: Monorail to Magic Kingdom, Contemporary Resort, the Transportation and Ticketing Center (TTC), EPCOT and the Polynesian Village Resort. For EPCOT, change at the TTC.
**Room prices**: Standard rooms: $737 to $1155. 1-Bedroom Villas: $992-$1647, 2-Bedroom Villas are $1612 to $2558 per night.
**Activities**: Arts and crafts, storytime, afternoon tea, Floridian Express guided tour for $15, princess promenade, character dinners, silhouette cut-outs for $15-$24, two pools – one with a waterslide and a water play area, electrical water pageant viewing, tennis courts, boat rentals, jogging, volleyball, spa and a 24-hour gym, and croquet.
**Extras**: Valet parking is $33 plus a tip. There are six shops in the main building. The Villas at Grand Floridian are also available to stay at. Accommodation includes studios, 1-bedroom and 2-bedroom apartments (sleeping up to 8 people).

## DINING

**1900 Park Fare** – Character Buffet, DDP, Breakfast – adults $45, children $29, Character Dinner – adults $60, children $39.
**Beach Pool Bar** – Pool Bar with Quick Service options, entrées at $11-$16 and drinks, DDP.
**Citricos** – Signature Table Service, DDP (2 Table Service credits), entrées are $33-$53.
**Courtyard Pool Bar** – Pool Bar with Snacks, serves entrees at $9-$11 and drinks, No DDP.
**Garden View Tea Room** – Afternoon Tea, No DDP, tea meals are $35-$50 for adults with a deluxe sharing tea at $150 for 2 people, a children's tea meal is priced at $23.
**Gasparilla Grill and Games** – Snacks and Quick Service, DDP, entrées are $8-$13.
**Grand Floridian Café** – Table Service, DDP, entrées $11-$27 at brunch, $16-$34 at dinner.
**Mizner's Lounge** – Drinks Lounge, No DDP. Appetizers are $13-$18.
**Narcoossee's** – Signature Table Service, DDP (2 Table Service credits), entrées are $34-$54.
**Perfectly Princess Tea Party** – Character lunch, No DDP, $334 for one adult and one child, then $235 per child and $99 per adult. Includes tea and cakes for two, a princess meet, other entertainment, and gifts for each child. Ages 4 to 12, targeted at girls - boys are welcome and receive different gifts. 10:30am to 12:00pm daily except Tues & Thur.
**Victoria and Albert's (Main Dining Room)** – Signature Dining, No DDP. A 7-course menu is $185, plus $65 for wine pairings. A 10-course menu is $235 ($340-$385 with wine).
**Victoria and Albert's Queen Victoria Room** – Signature Dining, No DDP. Prix Fixe menu at $235 for 10 courses, and an extra $150 when paired with wine.
**Victoria and Albert's Chef's Table** – Signature Dining, 9-10 course meal inside the Kitchen at Victoria and Albert's, No DDP. $250 per person ($355-$400 with wine pairings).
**Wonderland Tea Party at 1900 Park Fare** – Character lunch, cupcakes and tea, No DDP, $49.

# Polynesian Village Resort

With its Hawaiian theme and amazing location opposite Magic Kingdom, the 847-room Polynesian Village is our favorite deluxe resort.

The beach here is a key feature - it features panoramic views of Cinderella Castle and other nearby Disney resorts. You can lie on a hammock or a lounger and watch Magic Kingdom's fireworks.

While you cannot go into the lake, you can go inside the volcano-themed pool, just a short walk away.

You can also watch a torch lighting ceremony, enjoy the Electrical Water Pageant from the beach or take a boat to Magic Kingdom. This is what a vacation should be - immersive, luxurious, and laid-back.

**Transport**: Monorail to the Magic Kingdom, Contemporary Resort, Transportation and Ticketing Center (TTC), EPCOT and Polynesian Village Resort. For EPCOT, change monorail lines at the TTC. Buses serve all other parks. A boat is available to Magic Kingdom Park and the Grand Floridian resort. It is a 5-minute walk to the TTC. **Room size**: 409 ft$^2$.
**Room prices**: Standard rooms: $618 to $1053.

Bungalows: $3087-$5528.
**Activities**: A beach, water activities, two pools, waterfall and water slide, underwater jets, in-pool seating, jogging path. Boat rentals (extra fee). Use of the Grand Floridian's health club is complimentary. Check out the torch lighting ceremony five times a week, and the amazingly themed Trader Sam's bar.

## DINING

**Barefoot Pool Bar** – No Disney Dining Plan. Cocktails are $13-$15, beers are $7.50-$10.50.
**Captain Cook's** – Quick Service, DDP, entrées are $9.50-$12.50.
**Kona Café** – Table Service, DDP, entrées: $12-$16 at breakfast, $16-$36 at lunch & dinner.
**Kona Island Sushi** – Quick Service, No Disney Dining Plan, entrées are $15-$16.
**Oasis Bar and Grill** – Pool-side Bar and Quick Service, No DDP, entrées are $10-$17.
**Ohana** – Table Service, DDP, 'family-style' dinner, $55 for adults, $33 for children.
**Ohana's Best Friends Breakfast with Lilo & Stitch** – Character Buffet, DDP, $42 for adults, $27 for kids.
**Pineapple Lanai** – Serves dole whip ice creams at $5-$12, DDP.
**Spirit of Aloha Dinner Show at Luau Cove** – Dinner Show, Family Style Feast, DDP (2 Table Service credits), $66-$78 for adults, $39-$46 for kids, incl. tax and tip. 5:15pm to 8:00pm.
**Tambu Lounge** – Drinks, No Disney Dining Plan. Appetizers are $12-$18.
**Trader Sam's Grog Grotto** – Highly themed drinks lounge with snacks, No Disney Dining Plan. Ages 21+ only after 8:00pm. Cocktails are $12 to $32.

# Contemporary Resort

Located a five-minute walk from Magic Kingdom Park, this 750-room hotel boasts large standard rooms at 436ft$^2$, great dining options, and a modern theme.

The Contemporary Resort is a strange one: if you are looking for amazing theming then you will need to look elsewhere, but if you are looking for proximity to Magic Kingdom Park, a deluxe resort, and a wide range of amenities, then you need look no further.

Rooms at the resort are large and Guests who will base their stay around Magic Kingdom couldn't stay any closer to the park.

There are also many water recreation options available.

**Transport**: The monorail takes you directly to Magic Kingdom Park – or it is a 5-minute walk. EPCOT can be reached by monorail and changing lines at the Transportation and Ticketing Center. Monorail access to the Polynesian Village and Grand Floridian resorts. Wilderness Lodge and Fort Wilderness are a boat ride away. There are bus services to Disney Springs, Animal Kingdom, Hollywood Studios, and the water parks.

**Room prices**: Standard rooms are $518 to $882 per night. Rooms in the main resort building cost around an extra $200 per night. Bay Lake Tower rooms are $608 to $1011 per night for a studio, $889 to $1421 for a 1-Bedroom Villa and $1168 to $2468 for a 2-Bedroom Villa.

**Activities**: A fitness center, an arcade, basketball, volleyball, golf, and tennis courts.

---

## DINING

**California Grill** – Signature Restaurant, DDP (2 Table Service credits), entrées are $23-$59. Great views of fireworks. Sunday Brunch: $95 per adult (with 1 cocktail) & $56 per child.
**Chef Mickey's Buffet** – Character Buffet, DDP, breakfast and brunch are $50 per adult, $33 per child; dinner is $60 per adult, $39 per child. No characters during COVID-19 changes.
**Contempo Café** – Snacks and Quick Service, entrées are $11.50-$13, DDP.
**Cove Bar** – Pool Bar, DDP for food. Serves light snacks and drinks.
**Outer Rim** – Bar, No DDP. Serves drinks.
**Sand Bar** – Pool Bar, DDP for food. Offers Quick Service meals & drinks from $7.50-$13.
**The Wave** – Table Service, DDP, entrées are $12-$19 at breakfast & lunch, $18-$34 at dinner.

---

# Fort Wilderness Resort & Campground

This resort is split into 788 campsites in the Value range, the 409 cabins in the Moderate category.

Fort Wilderness is a real campground just a boat ride away from Magic Kingdom Park. The resort is an unapologetically authentic camping experience. It is probably not for you if you want a spa, hotel towels, or 24-hour room service.

At the most basic you have a campsite where you can bring your RV and tents and camp out under the stars or in your vehicle. Here you have shared shower and restroom facilities and must provide your own towels and toiletries. If you are the outdoorsy-type this could be perfect.

Alternatively, a big step up is the Wilderness Cabins which are just like many of Disney's hotel rooms but in individual units.

At the resort, there are countless outdoor activities and sports and several of our favorite dining experiences are here such as the *Hoop Dee Doo Musical Revue*

**Location**: In a forest between Magic Kingdom and EPCOT.
**Transport**: Due to the sheer size of this resort hotel (it is in a 750-acre forest), there is an internal bus system. For Magic Kingdom, take the boat from the marina. There are buses to the other parks and Disney Springs. You can also rent a golf cart for $59 plus tax per day (we suggest

pre-booking these).
**Room size**: Wilderness Cabins are 504 ft$^2$, 12' wide x 42' long. Campsite spaces are 25' wide and vary between 25' and 65' in length.
**Room prices**: $89 to $250 per night per campsite, $414-$789 per cabin.
**Activities**: Horse and pony rides, a petting farm, bike rentals, a 2.3-mile jogging trail, beach volleyball, basketball, shuffleboard, tetherball, and nature walks.

## DINING

**Hoop-Dee-Doo Musical Revue** – Family style feast with live entertainment, DDP (2 Table Service credits). Three categories of seating. Adults: $66-$74 and children: $39-$44.
**Meadow Snack Bar** – Snacks and Quick Service, DDP, entrées: $8-$10.50. Open seasonally.
**Trail's End Restaurant** – Breakfast and Dinner Buffet, DDP, the breakfast buffet is $27 per adult and $15 per child, the weekend brunch menu is $33 per adult and $18 per child, and the dinner buffet is $40 per adult and $22 per child.

# Old Key West Resort

Old Key West is in the deluxe villa category, offering a home away from home. The 709-room resort is themed to turn-of-the-century Key West.

Accommodations are among the largest at Walt Disney World. The resort is also often discounted so you can get a great deal.

The fact it is a large resort with so many amenities may be an inconvenience to guests - especially those using the Disney buses to get around. There are five bus stops within the resort, so remember which one is closest to your room.

For such a large resort, food options are limited. This is likely because all the rooms have kitchen facilities. However, Disney Springs is a short boat ride away with an abundance of dining.

**Location**: Between EPCOT and Disney Springs.
**Transport**: Buses to all Walt Disney World destinations. There is also a water ferry to Disney Springs.
**Room size**: Studio: 376 ft$^2$, 1 Bedroom: 942 ft$^2$, 2 Bedrooms: 1,333 ft$^2$, Grand Villa: 2,022 ft$^2$.
**Room prices**: Studio: $429-$705, 1 Bedroom: $584-1000, 2 Bedroom: $835-$1563. Rates for Grand Villas are $1785 to $2801.
**Activities**: Four pools, a beach, volleyball courts,

watercraft rentals, a jogging trail, bike rentals, arcades, basketball courts, shuffleboard, a fitness center, tennis courts, video rentals, air hockey, pool, darts, poolside movies, and bingo.
**Extras**: Ask for a "Hank's Happenings" newsletter to take a look at all the fun additional daily offerings that take place throughout the resort.

## DINING

**Good's Food To Go** – Snacks and Quick Service, entrées are $8-$12, DDP.
**Gurgling Suitcase** – Poolside bar and Quick Service, entrées are $8.50-$10.50, DDP.
**Olivia's Café** – Table Service, DDP, entrées are $15-$37 at lunch and dinner, and $14-$16 at breakfast.
**Turtle Shack Poolside Snacks** – Bar and Quick Service, DDP, entrées are $8-$12.

# Saratoga Springs Resort

Saratoga Springs is in the deluxe villa category and in many ways mirrors Old Key West Resort. This 1260-room resort in themed to Saratoga Springs is upstate New York.

Saratoga Springs is very

similar to Old Key West, although this resort has slightly smaller rooms.

As the accommodations all have cooking facilities, dining options are limited. You are, however, just a short boat ride away from

Disney Springs' food options.

The Treehouse Villas are unique to this resort: these villas are elevated 10 feet off the ground, offering great surrounding views and allowing you to feel immersed in nature - a truly unique experience.

**Location**: Disney Springs resort area.
**Transport**: Buses to all Walt Disney World locations, except Disney Springs where a boat service is available.
**Room size**: Studio – 355 ft² (up to 4 guests), 1-bedroom – 714 ft² (up to 4 guests), 2-bedrooms – 1075 ft² (up to 8 guests), 3-bedroom treehouse villas - 1074 ft²

(up to 9 guests), Grand Villa – 2113 ft² (up to 12 guests).
**Room prices**: Studio: $430-$701, 1-bedroom: $583-$991, 2-bedroom: $834-$1557, Treehouse Villas: $1043-$1942. Rates for the Grand Villas are $1785 to $2793 per night.
**Activities**: A pool with a waterslide, two whirlpools and an interactive children's play area, an arcade, tennis courts and bicycle rentals.

**Extras**: Senses – a full-service spa and health club (book on 407-WDW-SPAS).

## DINING

**Artist's Palette** – Quick Service, DDP, entrees: $7-$23 at breakfast, lunch & dinner $10-$13
**Backstretch Pool Bar** – Bar (Seasonal), Snacks and Ice Creams, DDP, sandwiches $8.50
**On the Rocks Pool Bar** – Bar, no DDP, serves drinks - no snacks
**Paddock Grill** – Quick Service, DDP at breakfast, entrees are $11-$13
**Sassagoula Pizza Express** – Pizza Delivery. Pizzas are $16-$18 plus 18% tip and tax
**Turf Club Bar and Grill** – Table Service, DDP, entrees are $20-$36.

# On-Site Non-Disney Hotels

Several hotels are *not* run by Disney but *are* on Disney property. The differences between these hotels and Disney hotels are generally the following:

•No Extra Magic Hours (extended theme park hours), with few exceptions.
• No Disney Dining Plans.
• Complimentary transportation between the hotels and the theme parks, although it runs less often than at Disney's hotels.

• No complimentary Disney Magical Express airport transportation.
• Prices are generally lower than at Disney hotels.
• Theming is non-existent.
•Some hotels charge extra resort fees - we have included these.
• Many of these hotels are part of major chains allowing you to redeem loyalty points.
Unfortunately, there are no advertised room rates for these resorts, so prices

listed are average nightly prices for an example trip booked 8 months in advance for June 1-6, 2021 based on 2 adults and 2 children (under 10) in a room. These prices will be than usual lower due to COVID-19.

We would recommend these on-site hotels over off-site hotels due to their location and transportation offerings.

# Doubletree by Hilton Orlando - Disney Springs

**Location**: Disney Springs area.
**Transport**: Free shuttle service to Walt Disney World theme parks, water parks and Disney Springs. Can also walk to Disney Springs.
**Number of rooms**: 229
**Room size**: Standard room is

350 ft², up to 850 ft² for 2-bed suites.
**Room prices**: $115 per night.
**Activities**: Pool, whirlpool, splash pad, tennis court and gym.
**Extras**: All rooms are suites with bedrooms, plus a separate living area. There is

a 5% AAA discount. Parking is $22 per night including tax. Breakfast is included in most rates.

**Dining**: *Evergreen Café* - Breakfast buffet, lunch and dinner table service. A lounge and poolside bar are also available.

# Walt Disney World Swan & Dolphin Resorts

Of all the non-Disney, on-site hotels, these resorts are is the closest to being a fully-fledged Disney resort.

The Swan Resort and Dolphin Resort are sister resorts located just across the water from each other.

**Location**: Between EPCOT and Disney's Hollywood Studios.
**Transport**: Boats to Disney's Hollywood Studios and EPCOT, or a 15-minute walk. Buses to other Walt Disney World locations.
**Number of rooms**: 756 (swan) and 1509 (dolphin)
**Room size**: 340 ft$^2$ (swan) and 360 ft$^2$ (dolphin)
**Room prices**: Around $295

including taxes and resort fees.
**Activities**: Several pools, four whirlpools, boat rentals, volleyball courts, gym, and spa.
**Extras**: Both these hotels offer Extra Magic Hours (extended theme park hours) – a benefit usually only Disney hotel guests get. Suites are available. Wi-Fi is included. Hotel parking is $27 per day, plus tax.

**Dining**:
*Garden Grove (Swan)*– Table Service
*Il Mulino (Swan)*– Table Service
*Kimonos: Sushi and Rolls (Swan)* – Table Service, sushi
*Cabana Bar and Grill*

*(Dolphin)*– Quick Service
*Fresh Mediterranean Market (Dolphin)* – Breakfast and Lunch. Buffet and a la carte options.
*Picabu Buffetaria (Dolphin)* – Quick Service
*Shula's Steak house (Dolphin)* – Table Service
*The Dolphin Fountain* – Quick Service
*Todd English's Bluezoo (Dolphin)* – Table Service

# Best Western Lake Buena Vista

**Location**: Disney Springs area.
**Transport**: Buses to all Walt Disney World theme parks every 30 minutes. Can walk to Disney Springs.
**Number of rooms**: 325
**Room size**: 325-345 ft$^2$.
**Room prices**: $149 per night.
**Activities**: Heated outdoor pool, children's pool, fitness center and an arcade.
**Extras**: Free Wi-Fi and self-parking, official Disney

souvenir shop, convenience store, laundry facility, transportation to Premium Outlets, complimentary newspapers (Mon-Fri) and a car rental desk. Room service is available. AAA discount is available (about 15%). Breakfast is included in most room rates.

**Dining**:
*Trader's Island Grill* – Buffet and Table Service, serves breakfast and dinner.

*Flamingo Cove Lounge*
*Marketplace* – Convenience store with grab-and-go eating options.

# Holiday Inn Orlando - Disney Springs

**Location**: Disney Springs area.
**Transport**: Complimentary shuttle to Disney Theme Parks every 30 minutes. Typhoon Lagoon, Blizzard Beach & Disney Springs buses run on a scheduled basis.

**Number of rooms**: 323
**Room prices**: $148 per night.
**Activities**: Gym, outdoor pool, games room,
**Extras**: Self-parking is $20 per night. Wi-Fi in all rooms. Breakfast is usually included in the room price. There are

on-site laundry facilities.
**Dining**:
*Palm Breezes Restaurant* – A fresh approach to classic American recipes. Serves Breakfast and Dinner only.
*Grab and Go* – Quick Service outlet.
*Palm Breezes Bar* – Bar.

# Shades of Green

**Location**: Magic Kingdom area.
**Theme**: Upscale Country Club.
**Transport**: Complimentary transportation to the Disney theme parks. Affordable paid transportation is available to SeaWorld and Universal Orlando.
**Number of rooms**: 586
**Room size**: 480 ft².
**Room prices**: From $139 per night
**Activities**: Magnolia Spa, 2 PGA golf courses surround this resort, gym, arcade, two pools, tennis courts and a playground.
**Extras**: Extra Magic Hours.

An exclusive resort for the military, their families and select other service members – details are available at shadesofgreen.org.

Upon check-in, a valid military ID or DOD ID, and current Leave and Earnings Statement (LES) are required. Room rates are based on military rank or civilian grade at the time of check-in.

**Dining:**
*Mangino's* – Fine dining.
*The Garden Gallery* – Table Service family restaurant.
*Express Cafe* – Quick Service restaurant.
*Java Cafe* – Serves Starbucks coffee and pastries.
*America, The Ice Cream Parlor* – 1950s themed ice cream parlor.

# Hilton Orlando Buena Vista Palace Disney Springs

**Location**: Disney Springs area.
**Transport**: Complimentary shuttle to Disney Theme Parks every 30 minutes. Typhoon Lagoon, Blizzard Beach & Disney Springs buses run on a scheduled basis.
**Number of rooms**: 1014
**Room size**: 400 ft².

**Room prices**: $248 per night.
**Activities**: Gym, spa and salon, heated swimming pools, tennis and basketball courts, and a treasure hunt.
**Extras**: In-room refrigerator. Suites, room service and babysitting are available. Parking is $22 per day.

**Dining:**
*Citrus 28* - Quick snacks and Starbucks coffee.
*Letterpress* - Table service restaurant. Buffet breakfast with Disney characters on Sunday.
*Shades* - Poolside bar with quick bites.
*Sunnies* - Lobby bar.

# Four Seasons Orlando

**Location**: Golden Oak community/EPCOT-Magic Kingdom area.
**Transport**: Coaches every 30 minutes to Magic Kingdom Park, and every hour to the other 3 theme parks.
**Number of rooms**: 443 guestrooms (including 68 suites)
**Room size**: Standard rooms start at 500 ft².
**Room prices**: $799 per night.
**Activities**: Treatments at 'The Spa', a variation of the Bibbidi Bobbidi Boutique called Magical Moments, several pools including a small water park and 11,000 ft² lazy river, 18-hole golf, on-site tennis courts, gym and sauna, and free Kids' Camp.
**Extras**: Next-day in-room merchandise delivery is available. Wi-Fi is free. Complimentary flavored water and sunscreen are available throughout the resort. There is a late departure lounge with amenities such as Wi-Fi. Valet parking is $30 per night - there is no self-parking available.

**Dining:**
*Ravello Lounge* – Bar
*Ravello Restaurant* – Modern Italian restaurant

with character dining breakfast option on Thursdays and Sundays.
*PB+G* – Casual food
*Lickety Split* – Dessert and coffee location
*Plancha* – Cuban American table service location
*Capa* – Contemporary Spanish steakhouse.

# Hilton Orlando Lake Buena Vista - Disney Springs

**Location**: Disney Springs area.
**Transport**: Complimentary transportation to all parks.
**Number of rooms**: 814
**Room prices**: $218 per night.
**Activities**: 24-hour gym center, two heated outdoor pools including a children's spray pool, and jogging trails.
**Extras**: Business center, valet parking ($30 per night), and self-parking ($22 per night). The resort fee

includes complimentary Wi-Fi and two selected beverages per day, unlimited movie rentals, a coffee maker and a refrigerator. A Disney Character Breakfast is available on Sundays. As well as regular rooms, junior suites and 1 and 2-bedroom suites are also available.

**Dining:**
*24-Hour Main Street Market* – Breakfast, lunch and dinner snacks. Serves

Starbucks coffee.
*Andiamo Italian Bistro* – Freshly prepared house specialties.
*Benihana Steakhouse and Sushi* – Table Service restaurant.
*Covington Mill* – Serves soups, salads, sandwiches and signature dishes.
*John TS* – Drinks Lounge. Serves salads, starters, entrées and sandwiches.
*Rum Largo Poolside Bar and Café* – Bar. Serves salads, starters and sandwiches.

# B Resort & Spa

**Location**: Disney Springs area.
**Transport**: Complimentary shuttle to Disney Parks every 30 minutes. Typhoon Lagoon, Blizzard Beach & Disney Springs buses run on a scheduled basis.
**Number of rooms**: 394
**Room prices**: $180 per night.
**Activities**: 24-hour gym, pool with interactive water elements, private cabanas and outdoor fire pits, ice cream parlor and gift shop, kids zone, spa, a hair salon,

relaxation lounge, and tennis courts.
**Extras**: Wi-Fi is available. There are courtesy iPads available at the front desk for guest use. 24-hour in-room dining. Suites. Self-parking is $23 and valet is $29.

**Dining**:
*American Q* – Classic American barbeque. The buffet is priced at $35 – a la carte mains are also available.
*Pickup* – A traditional grab-

n-go including an ice cream window service.
*Poolside bar and lounge* – Drinks lounge.

# Off-Site Hotels

The greater Orlando area contains approximately 450 hotels and 115,200 hotel guestrooms.

There are also more than 26,000 vacation home rentals available and more than 20,000 vacation ownership units.

As such, due to the huge number of off-site hotels, we cannot cover them in

this guide. We prefer to focus on the on-site official and partner hotels.

A popular area to stay is Orlando outside of Disney property is International Drive and its hotels - these hotels are a good mid-point between Walt Disney World and the Universal Orlando resort if you will be visiting both.

# Tickets
## Understanding Ticket Types

A basic ticket is called a *Base Ticket*. This allows you entry into one park per day. You cannot change parks on the same day. For example, if you wanted to visit EPCOT and then go to Magic Kingdom Park on the same day, a base ticket would not allow you to do this. A *Park Hopper* add-on to your ticket allows entry into all the theme parks, and you can go between them as many times as you want, including visiting multiple parks on the same day.

The *Park Hopper Plus* add-on to your ticket allows you a certain number of entries into Blizzard Beach water park, Typhoon Lagoon water park, ESPN Wide World of Sports Complex, a round of mini-golf at Fantasia Gardens (before 4:00 pm), a round of mini-golf at Winter Summerland (before 4:00 pm), or a round of golf at Oak Trail family walking course.

## Buying Tickets at the Gates

If you are having a spontaneous trip and wait until you get to the parks' turnstiles to buy your tickets, you pay the full rate. We recommend booking online before you go - you will save both time and money.

Ticket prices vary depending on a prediction of how busy the parks will be during your stay. The busier the parks, the more expensive tickets are.
Prices of discounted online tickets are on the next page. Tax (at 6.5%) is included.

For tickets of at least 3 days in length, there is a $21.30 discount for tickets bought online versus the gate prices - if you plan to buy at the park gates, add $21.30 to the prices on the next page for tickets over 3 days in length.

**Note**: There are no ticket booths at the Magic Kingdom Park gates; tickets must be bought at Guest Relations at Magic Kingdom Park's entrance, at the Transportation and Ticket Center, from another Disney park's ticket booths, or a Disney hotel.

Florida residents get discounts on gate prices with a Floridian ID when purchasing tickets. These tickets can only be purchased at the Walt Disney World Resort and not in advance.

## Disney's Ultimate Tickets - Europe Only

European residents have a few exclusive ticket options available, as many guests who visit Florida stay for 7, 14, or 21 days. Standard tickets cannot accommodate visits of these lengths.

On the official Disney website, a 7-day ticket for 2021 is priced at £439 per adult and £419 per child. A 14-day ticket is £479 and £459. You can often find these tickets cheaper from resellers other than Disney.

Disney's Ultimate Tickets allow you unlimited entry into the theme parks, entertainment complexes, water parks, and mini golf courses, and also include photos with Memory Maker.

There are often promotions offering a 14-day ticket for the price of a 7-Day Premium Ticket if staying at a Disney resort.

# Online

The official website to purchase your Walt Disney World tickets from is disneyworld.Disney.com. The online pricing can be seen on the next page.

Many online ticket resellers offer tickets at reduced prices. Be sure to buy from a reputable seller.

UnderCoverTourist.com, for example, has up to $65 off some Disney World tickets. We are not able to recommend any companies specifically.

# Online Ticket Pricing

|  | Base Ticket (Adult/Child) | Base Ticket + Park Hopper (Adult/Child) | Base Ticket + Park Hopper Plus (Adult/Child) |
|---|---|---|---|
| 1 Day | $116-$169/$111-$164 | $185-$238/$180-$233 | $206-$259/$201-$254 |
| 2 Days | $226-$330/$216-$319 | $306-$410/$296-$399 | $327-$431/$317-$421 |
| 3 Days | $336-$476/$321-$461 | $416-$556/$401-$541 | $437-$577/$422-$562 |
| 4 Days | $435-$597/$416-$578 | $525-$687/$507-$669 | $547-$709/$528-$690 |
| 5 Days | $464-$631/$443-$611 | $554-$721/$534-$701 | $575-$743/$555-$723 |
| 6 Days | $478-$646/$457-$625 | $568-$736/$547-$716 | $590-$758/$569-$737 |
| 7 Days | $492-$662/$470-$640 | $583-$752/$561-$730 | $604-$773/$582-$752 |
| 8 Days | $518-$679/$496-$656 | $609-$769/$586-$747 | $630-$791/$607-$768 |
| 9 Days | $536-$692/$513-$669 | $626-$782/$603-$759 | $647-$804/$625-$781 |
| 10 Days | $554-$704/$530-$680 | $644-$794/$620-$770 | $666-$815/$642-$792 |

Prices are seasonal and vary based on the dates of your visit. Prices presented here are for tickets purchased online or when booking a package through Disney including a hotel and tickets - add $21.30 to tickets at least 3 days long if buying at the theme park gates. These prices listed are rounded to the nearest dollar.

You can also buy tickets at any Disney Store for the Walt Disney World Resort at the same prices available at the gate. This will save you time waiting in a queue line on your first day. In the UK, you can only buy "Disney's Ultimate" tickets at the stores.

# Ticket Tips

•You will need at least 2 days to tour Magic Kingdom Park, 2 days for EPCOT, 1 day for Disney's Hollywood Studios, and 1 day for Animal Kingdom. More time allows for a more relaxed pace, which we are sure you will appreciate while on vacation. To see all four parks and their attractions, you will need an absolute minimum of 6 days on your ticket, in our opinion, although if you only want to see the highlights then one day at each park is enough.

•There are free admission shopping, dining, and entertainment areas at the Walt Disney World Resort such as Disney Springs and The Boardwalk.

•Check out disneyworld.Disney.go.com/special-offers/ for special offers on tickets and hotels, including free tickets and free nights.

•If you are planning on making multiple visits to Walt Disney World within one year, it can pay to purchase an annual pass.

# Magic Kingdom Park

*Disney's Magic Kingdom Park* is the most visited theme park in the world with 21 million visitors in 2019. Magic Kingdom Park was the first theme park built at Walt Disney World.

**An important note on Parking:**
Guests arriving at *Magic Kingdom Park* by car, park at the *Transportation and Ticket Center (TTC)* parking lots. Once parked, you either catch a tram or walk to the TTC.

Then, either catch the Monorail or the Ferryboat. A bus option is also occasionally offered. Within less than 10 minutes, you will be at the entrance to the Magic Kingdom. During peak season, you will have to wait in a queue line to board the monorail or a ferry here.

The parking lots for all the other theme parks at the Walt Disney World Resort are located by the park entrances.

Parking is charged at the following rates (per day): Cars or Motorbikes - $25. Taxis, Limos, Campers, Trailers, RVs, buses, or Tractor Trailers - $30. Preferred parking is $50.

Disney resort hotel guests can waive the parking fee by scanning their MagicBand at the parking toll plazas. Guests arriving by resort transportation (bus, monorail, or boat) arrive directly at the entrance to Magic Kingdom.

## ✿ COVID-19 CHANGES:

At the moment as well as needing a park ticket, you also **need a Park Pass Reservation** for the first park you wish to visit each day - do this at DisneyWorld.com. **Face coverings are required** for guests ages 2 and up at all times at the parks except when eating while stationary. **Guests will be temperature screened** to enter the park. At the time of writing **all parades, shows and fireworks are suspended. FastPass+ and Single Rider lines are suspended at all parks.** Other offerings may be reduced or suspended.

## Attraction Key

In the park chapters, we list each attraction individually along with some key information. Here are what the symbols in the next sections mean.

| | | | |
|---|---|---|---|
|  | Does it have FastPass+? |  | Minimum Height (inches) |
|  | Is there an on-ride photo? |  | Ride/Show Length |
|  | Average wait time (on peak days) | | |

# Main Street, U.S.A.

*When you walk into the park, Main Street, U.S.A. is the first thing you will see. Most guests simply refer to this as 'Main Street'.*

Main Street, U.S.A. is inspired by Walt Disney's hometown of Marceline, Missouri and is themed to recreate a turn-of-the-20th-century street.

Main Street, U.S.A. features shops on both sides of the street and leads to Cinderella Castle at the end. From this 'hub' area in front of the castle, you can venture into one of six themed lands. Due to its location, you will pass Main Street both when entering and exiting the park.

Main Street opens to guests approximately 1 hour before the official park opening time. This means you can enter Main Street and shop and dine before exploring the rest of the park. Five minutes before the park's scheduled opening time, a show 'Let the Magic Begin' is performed in front of Cinderella Castle to officially

open the park.

**City Hall** is immediately to the left before entering Main Street, U.S.A. This is the one-stop-shop for pins, badges, help, disability cards, positive feedback and complaints.

For shopping, the main store here is the huge **Emporium,** but there are many smaller niche stores too along both sides of the street.

## WHAT IS FASTPASS+?

A free time-saving service that allows you to reserve a time to ride an attraction instead of waiting in a queue line. It is currently suspended due to COVID-19.

The **Main Street Chamber of Commerce** is where you can pick up items that you buy during the day instead of carrying them around the park.

In addition to the attractions listed on the next page, you can enjoy **Harmony Barber Shop** (a real barbershop - reservations are highly recommended at 407-W-DISNEY) and the **Main Street Vehicles**, which you can ride up and down Main Street, U.S.A. if you prefer to give your feet a rest.

## Sorcerers of the Magic Kingdom

This is an interactive card game where you venture from land to land in the Magic Kingdom finding portals. Once at a portal, hold up your magic game

cards and screens will activate. Your cards will then help you defeat the Disney villains.

The more you play, the harder it gets, so you can progress throughout your trip. To play, simply pick up your complimentary playing cards from the Firehouse on Main Street, U.S.A. Here you are given a map and full instructions.

Guests can add five new random cards to add to their roster each day.

## Town Square Theater

**Fastpass+**: Yes

Meet Mickey Mouse backstage at the Town Square Theater and create memories that last a lifetime. While you are at it, grab some photos too!

Surprisingly, the wait time is rarely above 30 minutes.

Other characters also meet at this location periodically.

# Main Street U.S.A. Railroad Station

Hop aboard the Walt Disney World Railroad for a circular tour around Magic Kingdom Park on a classic steam locomotive.

The Railroad is a relaxing way to get around the park with several stations. At each of these stations, you can get on or off - the other stations are located in Frontierland and Fantasyland.

| No | None | No | Up to 20 mins | Under 10 mins |

The full tour of the park takes approximately 20 minutes to complete, with trains every five minutes or so, but you are free to get on and off at whichever station you want. You can also stay on all the way around if you wish.

The Railroad does not operate during parades as the floats need to cross its tracks to access the main park areas. The Railroad is suspended during *TRON Lightcycle Run* construction.

## DINING

**Casey's Corner** - Quick Service, DDP accepted, entrées are $9.50-$13.50.
**The Crystal Palace** - Character Buffet, DDP accepted, $42 for adults and $27 for kids at breakfast; $55 per adult and $36 per child at lunch and dinner.
**Main Street Bakery** - Quick Service, DDP accepted, serves Starbucks products and bakery goods, sandwiches are $7, drinks are $3.50-$6.
**Plaza Ice Cream Parlor** - Snacks, No DDP, ice creams are $7-$7.50.
**The Plaza Restaurant** - Table Service, DDP accepted, entrées are $14-$18 at breakfast and $17-$21 at lunch and dinner.

# Frontierland

## Big Thunder Mountain Railroad

Jump aboard a family rollercoaster sure to bring a smile to everyone's face.

This ride lasts about just under 4 minutes, which is unusually long for a coaster.

As you venture through the mine, you will see geysers, dynamite, western towns, flooding caves, bats, and more!

The standby queue line (not Fastpass+) even has some interactive elements to help pass the time.

| FP | Yes | 📏 | 40" | 📷 | No | ⏱ | 4 mins | ⧗ | 90 to 120 mins |

This is a great family ride which is relatively tame as roller coasters go, and a way to get kids interested in riding something more exhilarating.

## Splash Mountain

Hop on a ride inspired by Br'er Rabbit's adventure and the *Song of the South* movie.

| FP | Yes | 📏 | 40" | 📷 | Yes | ⏱ | 7 mins | ⧗ | 90 to 120 mins |

*Splash Mountain* is a log flume-style ride with a long indoor portion with many colorful scenes. The ride is great fun with music, animatronics, and small indoor drops to enjoy along the way – then, as the action heats up, you plummet down a 52-foot drop at the end and discover why this is called *Splash Mountain*.

Surprisingly, you do not usually get very wet on this ride, it is more of a spray than a soak.

However, there is always a chance you will come out drenched so you will want to leave your electronics and valuables with a non-rider.

## Country Bear Jamboree

*Country Bear Jamboree* is a sit-down theater-show-style attraction with pre-recorded singing from a series of animatronic bears.

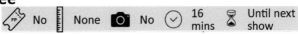

| FP | No | 📏 | None | 📷 | No | ⏱ | 16 mins | ⧗ | Until next show |

To be honest, it is probably our least favorite attraction in the Magic Kingdom as it is very outdated and has never resonated with us.

On the other hand, it does provide shelter from the rain and heat and allows for a sit-down break with no queue lines. Kids may also be amused.

Go in if you have the time, but do not make it a priority, and do not expect any miracles from the show.

---

### DINING

**Golden Oak Outpost** - Snacks, DDP accepted, nuggets and waffle fries are $6.50-$10
**Pecos Bill Tall Tale Inn and Cafe** - Quick Service, DDP accepted, entrées are $9.50-$15
**Westward Ho** - Snacks, DDP accepted, $9 for a corn dog, $3 for chips, and $3-$5 for drinks

# Liberty Square

## Haunted Mansion

*Haunted Mansion* is a beloved Disney classic that should not be missed.

Despite its name and its imposing facade, this is not a horror-maze or a horror ride – it is a gentle ride with tongue-in-cheek humor.

There are no jump scares but the spooky atmosphere and loud laughter during the initial section may frighten younger children, as well as the pop-up ghosts during the final scenes of the ride. You should also be aware that it is very dark inside.
Once you step foot into the

| | | | | | | | |
|---|---|---|---|---|---|---|---|
| 🎟️ FP | Yes | 📏 None | 📷 | No | ⏱️ | 8 mins | ⏳ 30 to 45 mins |

mansion and explore the entrance area, you will be lead to "Doom Buggies" to sit in. These are small vehicles that tilt and rotate as you go through various scenes of the mansion.

You will see ghosts dancing, singing busts, a ghostly seance, ravens and much more.

## The Hall of Presidents

This show features audio-animatronics of all 44 US presidents, as well as multimedia elements showcasing snippets of America's political history.

Children, and those who are

| | | | | | | | |
|---|---|---|---|---|---|---|---|
| 🎟️ | No | 📏 None | 📷 | No | ⏱️ | 22 mins | ⏳ Until next show |

less politically minded, are unlikely to be entertained. However, fierce patriots will likely enjoy the show.

The animatronics are incredibly advanced and are spookily life-like. The attraction features a speech from the US president.

## Liberty Square Riverboat

Sail around Tom Sawyer Island on a leisurely cruise on the Liberty Square Riverboat. There is a very limited amount of seating and most space is standing room on this cruise.

| | | | | | | | |
|---|---|---|---|---|---|---|---|
| 🎟️ FP | No | 📏 None | 📷 | No | ⏱️ | 13 mins | ⏳ Until next boat |

Closing times vary seasonally and a sign at the loading area will list the time of the day's last trip, as

well as the frequency of departures (usually every half hour).

---

### DINING

**Columbia Harbour House** - Snacks and Quick Service, DDP accepted, entrées are $9-$16

**The Diamond Horseshoe Revue** - Table Service, DDP accepted. The all-you-can-eat family-style meal is $39 per adult and $21 per child. Entrees are $17-$22.

**Liberty Tree Tavern** - Table Service, DDP accepted, entrées are $20-$24 for lunch and $39 for an all-you-can-eat family-style meal for adults and $21 for kids.

**Liberty Square Market** - Snacks, DDP accepted, hot dogs $8, turkey legs are $12.50

**Sleepy Hollow** - Snacks, DDP accepted, waffles:$7-$10.50, funnel cakes: $7, drinks: $3.50-$5.50

---

# Adventureland

## Pirates of the Caribbean

Ahoy me hearties! Set sail through the world of the 'Pirates of the Caribbean'.

Featuring the characters from the famous "Pirates of the Caribbean" blockbusters, as well as original characters that inspired the hit movies, this is a fun water flume ride through pirate-filled scenes with a small drop to add a thrill element too.

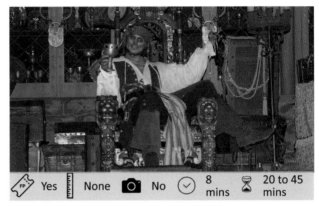

| FP Yes | None | 📷 No | ✓ 8 mins | ⧗ 20 to 45 mins |

Guests board boats and sail by scenes with amazing animatronic characters. Well-known songs are played throughout the attraction adding to the pirate-like atmosphere.

The original version of this ride in Disneyland was the final attraction Walt Disney supervised the creation, making this something truly special in the world of Disney theme parks.

## The Magic Carpets of Aladdin

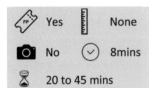

| FP Yes | None |
| 📷 No | ✓ 8mins |
| ⧗ 20 to 45 mins | |

Hop aboard one of Aladdin's magic carpets and fly across Adventureland. This is a gentle ride and is very similar to Dumbo in Fantasyland.

## Swiss Family Robinson Treehouse

This elaborately themed walkthrough attraction allows you to enter The Robinson's treehouse and venture from room to room seeing how they built their home following a shipwreck, making the most of nature around them.

There is no wait to explore this area and it is a good way to spend a few minutes.

## Enchanted Tiki Room

A Walt Disney original attraction, step into the frankly bewildering world of singing flowers and birds in the *Enchanted Tiki Room*.

It is perhaps Walt Disney World's most bewildering attraction, and in our opinion needs a replacement for today's generation.

## A Pirate's Adventure: Treasures of the Seven Seas

This interactive game will have you exploring Adventureland looking for hidden treasures as you take on one of the five tasks dotted around the land.

When you begin, you will receive a magic talisman, as well as a map to help you along your way finding treasure.

Once you have found a spot, touch your talisman and see how you change Adventureland around you.

Each mission lasts 15 to 20 minutes and it is a fun way to add a unique experience to your day without needing to wait in a queue line.

**Top Tip**: Complete 2 out of 5 missions and you will get a bonus FastPass+ for *Pirates of The Caribbean*.

## Jungle Cruise

| | | | | |
|---|---|---|---|---|
| FP Yes | None | No | 10 minutes | 45 to 90 minutes |

Jump aboard and set sail through jungles across the world, with a skipper who just cannot help but tell the corniest jokes you have ever heard. Along the way, you will see a variety of animatronic animals.

As each boat has its own individual skipper, the ride experience can really vary from an outrageously hilarious trip to one where the guide offers minimal enthusiasm.

The queue line is fairly tedious with nothing much to see or do, so we recommend you make a FastPass+ reservation for this attraction.

---

### DINING

**Aloha Isle** - Snacks, No DDP, dole whips and floats are $5-$7, drinks are $3.50-$4
**Jungle Navigation Co., Ltd. Skipper Canteen** - Table Service, DDP accepted, African, American, Asian and Latin cuisine, entrées are $19-$36
**Sunshine Tree Terrace** - Snacks, No DDP, desserts are $5-$7, drinks are $3.50-$4
**Tortuga Tavern** - Snacks & Quick Service, DDP accepted, American cuisine, entrées: $10-$15

# Fantasyland

## Cinderella Castle

Step inside Cinderella's castle and walk under the entranceway across the moat and into Fantasyland.

Standing at 189 feet tall, Cinderella Castle is the central icon of the Magic Kingdom and indeed the whole of Walt Disney World.

As you cross the drawbridge and walk through the castle, be sure to look at the incredibly detailed mosaics around you.

Unlike some of the other Disney castles such as those at Disneyland and Disneyland Paris, you cannot visit the area inside the castle upstairs. The only exception is if you are dining at the Cinderella's Royal Table restaurant which includes appearances from the Disney princesses and select other characters.

Inside the castle on the first floor, you will find the **Bibbidi Bobbidi Boutique**, a makeover salon, where little girls can be transformed into princesses complete with make-up, a Disney costume dress and a hairdo.

Packages for Bibbidi Bobbidi Boutique (suspended during COVID-19) vary between $65 and $450, plus tax, depending on what your princess chooses to do. Boys can take part in the form of the rather reasonably priced "Knight Package" for $20 plus tax. It includes hairstyling with gel, confetti, as well as a sword and shield to keep. A deluxe package is sold at $80.

Reservations can be made up to 180 days in advance and are strongly recommended by calling 407-WDW-STYLE or 407-939-7895.

## Prince Charming Regal Carrousel

|  No |  None |  No |  90 secs |  Less than 10 mins |
|---|---|---|---|---|

Ride a beautiful horse in the heart of the Magic Kingdom.

This is a beautiful vintage carousel, which pre-dates the Magic Kingdom and is now over 100 years old.

The carousel is fun to ride for every member of the family and wait times never seem to be more than 5 or 10 minutes.

For a different experience, visit the carousel at night and see it all lit up!

**Note:** This ride does not operate immediately before, during, or after any firework shows.

## Mad Tea Party

A standard fairground ride where you ride in a teacup and spin.

If you want to go faster, just turn the wheel in the center of the cup – you can reach some dizzying speeds.

The wait times are never too long for this attraction and if the posted wait is anything more than 15 minutes, we recommend you simply come back later in the day.

| | | | | | |
|---|---|---|---|---|---|
| Yes | None | No | 90 secs | Less than 5 mins |

## Princess FairyTale Hall

Meet and greet Disney princesses in this most royal of settings.

| | | | | | |
|---|---|---|---|---|---|
| Yes | None | Yes | 2 mins | 30 to 90 mins |

Choose one of the two queue lines: one is to meet Cinderella and a visiting princess; the other is to meet Rapunzel and a visiting princess.

The interior of the meet and greet is lavish with stone walls, chandeliers and Cinderella themed stained-glass windows in the queue line. You will even get a chance to see Cinderella's glass slipper!

## Casey Jr. Splash 'N' Soak Station

Located in the Storybook Circus area, this play area is a great place to cool down. There are streams of water from the giraffes and other animals and even a smoky mist from Casey Jr.'s chimney. As this is an open area, there is no wait to get in, making this the perfect place to let the young ones play.

## "it's a small world"

One of the most memorable attractions, *"it's a small world"* features hundreds of singing dolls singing a catchy tune about the uniting of the world.

Your cruise travels leisurely

| | | | | | |
|---|---|---|---|---|---|
| Yes | None | No | 10 mins | Less than 30 mins |

around scenes from across the world and this is a fun ride, especially for younger kids. The queue line for this ride moves very quickly.

This is a great Disney classic, which, although not based on any film franchise, is one of the many "must-dos" for most visitors.

## The Barnstormer

A small roller coaster for kids with one drop and a few turns.

The ride is good fun but it is very short, and rougher than it appears from the

| | | | | | |
|---|---|---|---|---|---|
| Yes | 35" | No | 1 min | 25 to 45 mins |

outside.

It is a good starter coaster for kids, and it has a very low minimum height limit meaning that almost anyone can enjoy it.

# Seven Dwarfs Mine Train

This fun rollercoaster contains both inside dark ride elements and outside rollercoaster sections taking you into the world of Snow White and even the Seven Dwarf's mine where "a million diamonds shine".

The ride cars swing as guests go around bends as real mine carts would. The thrill level is just below *Big Thunder Mountain* but a step up from The Barnstormer. It also fits

Yes | 38" | Yes | 3 mins | 90 to 120 mins

perfectly in the middle for the height limit – a true family ride.

# Under the Sea - Journey of the Little Mermaid

*Under the Sea* is our favorite classic-style dark ride at Walt Disney World as it is perfectly executed.

The storytelling is great, the animatronics are amazing, the music is exceptional. The ride entertains throughout while moving slowly and steadily enough to not frighten young ones.

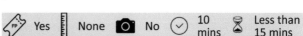
Yes | None | No | 5 mins | 20 to 45 mins

Watch out for the incredible appearance of Ursula if you have any sensitive guests in your group, although the moment is quickly over.

Even the queue line is fun with incredible theming,

character appearances from Scuttle, and an interactive game to play where you spot the crabs.

**Top Tip**: In the last hour of park operation, there is often no wait.

# Mickey's Philharmagic

*Philharmagic* is, in our opinion, by far Walt Disney World's best 4D show, and one that cannot be missed.

Here, you are attending Goofy's opera performance with Mickey's Philharmonic orchestra. When Donald gets involved, however, things get out of hand and

Yes | None | No | 10 mins | Less than 15 mins

you end up on an adventure traveling through a world of Disney classic movies.

With an air-conditioned queue line and theater, shelter from the rain, and a fantastic movie, it is easy to

see why this attraction has one of the highest guest ratings at Magic Kingdom.

**Top Tip**: At the end of the show, Donald flies off the screen - look at the back of the theater for a surprise.

# The Many Adventures of Winnie the Pooh

Hop inside one of Pooh's "hunny pots" and explore one of his many adventures.

This is a gentle ride where you venture through Pooh's

Yes | None | No | 3 mins | 45 to 75 mins

stories; it includes slight rocking and jumping motions to enhance the experience.

As well as the popular characters, the ride is filled with bright colors that should excite the little ones.

# Enchanted Tales with Belle

An interactive adventure where you enter Maurice's cottage and are magically transported to the Beast's castle. Once there, you will meet Madame Wardrobe and have a chance to surprise Belle!

Not everyone in the group must take part in surprising Belle, but you can volunteer to help if you want. If you

 Yes | None |  Yes | 15 mins | 30 to 60 mins

do not wish to, you can sit back and enjoy the show.

Even if you do not fancy meeting the princesses, we highly recommend visiting this attraction – it is definitely worth the wait and the attraction includes some incredible special

effects too.

**Top Tip**: Make sure you get a good view of the mirror behind the Cast Member at the start! The Lumière animatronic in the main show room is not to be missed either.

# Peter Pan's Flight

*Peter Pan's Flight* is one of the Magic Kingdom's most popular rides. You board a flying pirate ship and take a voyage through the world of Peter Pan and Never Never Land.

The scenes are both beside you and below you, and the interior of this ride is stunning, from the moment you step in.

 Yes |  None |  No | 5 mins | 90 to 120 mins

This ride is incredibly popular, so a FastPass+ reservation is a must.

The low capacity of the ride, coupled with the popularity of the characters, causes long waits to form. However, guests in the standby line enjoy a

fantastic interactive queue line that takes you through the Darlings' nursery.

**Note**: If you are afraid of heights, this ride may not be suitable as the ships give the sensation of flight. At times you are several feet off the ground.

# Dumbo: The Flying Elephant

Dumbo is one of the most popular rides at Magic Kingdom Park. As you gently spin, use the lever at front of the seats in each Dumbo elephant to lift yourself up or down!

When you are in-flight, the ride offers nice views of the

Yes | None |  No |  90 secs | 20 to 45 mins

surrounding area, as well as a whole lot of fun.

Due to its popularity, there are now two sets of Dumbos. Disney uses a clever waiting system where

you are given a pager. Kids can play in an indoor air-conditioned play area - once it is your turn to board, you are paged. You forget you are waiting in line!

---

## DINING

**Be Our Guest Restaurant** - Quick Service [breakfast and lunch] and Table Service [2 credits - dinner], DDP accepted – the breakfast prix fixe meal is $29 for adults and $16 for children, lunch entrées are $15-$19, dinner prix fixe meals are $62 per adult and $37 per child. Reservations are required for all meals, including Quick Service.

**Cheshire Café** - Snacks, No DDP, Cheshire Cat tail snack - $5.50, drinks are $3.50-$5

**Cinderella's Royal Table** - Table Service, DDP accepted, breakfast prices are $62 per adult ($37 per child), lunch & dinner is $75 per adult and $4 per child.

**Gaston's Tavern** - Snacks, DDP accepted, snacks are $3.50-$10.50, & drinks are $3-$13

**Pinocchio Village Haus** - Snacks and Quick Service, DDP accepted, entrées are $10-$13.50.

**Prince Eric's Village Market** - Snacks, No DDP, snacks such as fruits & pretzels are $2-$10.

**Storybook Treats** - Snacks, No DDP, ice creams and floats are $5-$7.

**The Friar's Nook** - Quick Service, DDP accepted, entrees are $10-$11.

# Tomorrowland

## Buzz Lightyear Space Ranger Spin

Buzz Lightyear invites you to step aboard his ship and use the on-board blasters to help defeat the evil emperor Zurg. By shooting the targets around you, you will be helping out Buzz and racking up points.

Different targets are worth different amounts of points; there are even hidden targets to get thousands of bonus points in one go.

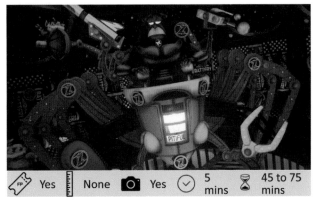

|  Yes | None  Yes | 5 mins | 45 to 75 mins |
|---|---|---|---|

You can also change the direction of your Space Cruiser with the joystick and turn the car the other way if you spot a target your friend has not. At the end of the ride, the one with the most points wins. It is competitive and endlessly 're-rideable'.

## Tomorrowland Transit Authority Peoplemover

One of our favorite hidden gems at the Magic Kingdom is the Peoplemover - a relaxing way to tour Tomorrowland including

|  No | None No | 10 mins | Less than 10 mins |
|---|---|---|---|

seeing the inside of *Space Mountain* and *Buzz Lightyear Space Ranger Spin!* The ten-minute ride is a chance to put up your feet.

## Monsters, Inc. Laugh Floor

Step in for an interactive show with Mike Wazowski and his comical friends from 'Monsters Inc.' who are ready to interact with the audience, including you.

|  Yes | None No | 12 mins | 15 to 30 mins |
|---|---|---|---|

Get ready to laugh, play, and potentially be made fun of.

You will want to be sure you are having fun or you might have the pleasure of being dubbed by the monsters as "That Guy" during the show.

## Tomorrowland Speedway

Little kids are notorious for loving little cars and this is their first chance to have a go driving for themselves. Here, you get to cruise along at up to 7mph and enjoy the

| Yes | See text | No | 5 mins | 30 to 60 mins |
|---|---|---|---|---|

sights.

The minimum height is 54"

to drive alone, and kids must be at least 32" tall to ride with an adult.

## Astro Orbiter

Above the Peoplemover is Astro Orbiter, a spinning type ride similar to *Dumbo The Flying Elephant*. The difference here is that these

| No | None | No | 90 secs | 25 to 45 mins |
|---|---|---|---|---|

rockets spin much faster, and you are much higher up.

**Note**: The space rockets are very small and getting two adults into one is tough!

## Space Mountain

*Space Mountain* is a roller coaster through space designed with the family in mind - it has no loops or inversions and provides the feeling of soaring through the galactic world.

We strongly recommend making a Fastpass+ reservation as the standby queue line is tedious. Alternatively, get to this ride first thing in the morning or at the end of the day to minimize your wait.

FP Yes | 40" | 📷 Yes | ⊘ 3 mins | ⧗ 90 to 120 *mins

## TRON Lightcycle Run [Expected to open in 2021]

On this high-speed rollercoaster, you sit forward in on a Lightcycle from the TRON franchise. This is coaster features a powerful launch that has you hitting speeds of 59mph. After a quick visit outside, you enter "the grid" where projections and other effects simulate a race between you and your opponents.

**Top Tip**: The restraint system may be uncomfortable (and restrictive) for some guests

FP Yes | 48" | 📷 ? | ⊘ 2 mins | ⧗ 120 to 180 mins

– the best way of describing it, is being on a motorbike

leaning forward traveling at high speed.

## Walt Disney's Carousel of Progress

A classic attraction designed by Walt Disney himself, the Carousel of Progress is a touching, funny, and heartwarming show that moves from scene to scene every few minutes.

FP No | None | 📷 No | ⊘ 20 mins | ⧗ Less than 10 mins

You start off seeing how life was like in the early 1900s, then every few minutes the carousel rotates and you move forward in time with the family by a few decades.

## DINING

**Auntie Gravity's Galactic Goodies** - Snacks, No DDP, ice creams: $5.50-$7, drinks: $3.50-$4
**Cool Ship** - Snacks, No DDP, drinks are $3-$5, a hot dog with chips is $9
**Cosmic Ray's Starlight Café** - Quick Service, DDP accepted, churros are $6.50
**The Lunching Pad** - Snacks and Quick Service, DDP accepted, entrées are $9.50-$13
**Tomorrowland Terrace Restaurant** - Snacks & Quick Service, DDP, entrées are $10.50-$13

# Live Entertainment

*Magic Kingdom Park has plenty of entertainment offerings throughout the day - this is all included in your park admission price and you could fill almost an entire day with the live entertainment alone.*

**Flag Retreat (Main Street, U.S.A.)** – Hear patriotic songs as the American flag is lowered and folded in the afternoon each day with the help of a guest – usually a service person or a veteran. Length: About 15 minutes.

**Citizens of Main Street** – Meet the citizens of Main Street, U.S.A., including the Mayor, the chief fireman, and other locals.

**Main Street Philharmonic at Main Street, U.S.A.** – This band plays Disney tunes.

**Main Street Trolley Show** – A 5-minute show around a horse-drawn streetcar. This usually takes place several times in the morning.

**Casey's Corner Pianist (Main Street, U.S.A.)** – Join the pianist at Casey's Corner and listen to his tunes. He even takes song requests.

**Main Street Philharmonic at Storybook Circus (Fantasyland)** – This classic band plays tunes from Disney movies.

**"A Totally Tomorrowland Christmas Show" (Tomorrowland – Holiday season only)** – Join this intergalactic Christmas party where Stitch jets off to find Santa. About 20 minutes.

**The Dapper Dans (Main Street, U.S.A.)** – Enjoy the live singing from this barbershop quartet.

## STAGE SHOWS

**Mickey's Royal Friendship Faire** – This 20-minute show features Mickey Mouse and his friends, along with characters from some of Disney's newest classics.

**A Frozen Holiday Wish (Holiday Season)** – See Cinderella's Castle be transformed into a glittering, icy palace with the help of Anna and Elsa.

**"Celebrate the Season" Show (Holiday season)** – This 25-minute show features Mickey and Minnie as they spread some holiday cheer, including Disney songs.

# Parades

**Disney's Festival of Fantasy Parade** is a must-watch; it is the park's main parade. It usually takes place at 2:00pm or 3:00pm daily and starts in Frontierland by *Splash Mountain*. It goes through Liberty Square, round the castle hub, and down Main Street, U.S.A.

The parade brings the magical stories of Fantasyland to life through parade floats, vibrant costumes, and an original soundtrack that features beloved songs from favorite Disney films.

Ariel and friends grace a larger-than-life music box

showcasing a musical party "Under the Sea", while Scottish dancers and a bagpipe-shaped float announce the arrival of Merida.

Other floats celebrate Disney Princesses and

Dumbo; Peter Pan and Wendy soar above a pirate galleon; a steampunk Maleficent float makings a stunning entrance, and Rapunzel and Flynn Rider appear too!

A Dining Package with

reserved parade viewing is available at Tony's Town Square Restaurant. At the cost of $54 for adults and $19 for children (ages 3-9), the package provides an enjoyable way to combine a meal and some entertainment.

**The Move It! Shake It! MousekeDance It! Street Party** happens up to three times a day with the main show taking place on the hub in front of Cinderella Castle. In this interactive parade, the floats stop and you get to join in with the dancing.

During the Halloween season, you can see Mickey's "Boo to You" Halloween Parade, and during the Holiday season there is a special parade too, Mickey's Once Upon a Christmastime Parade.

# Nighttime Spectacular

Every evening, experience a grand finale to your day with spectacular fireworks in *Happily Ever After*.

*Happily Ever After* starts with a dream... and takes you on a journey that captures the heart, humor, and heroism of Disney animated movies.

This 18-minute show features more lasers, lights, and projections than any other spectacular in the Magic Kingdom's history!

Get a spot in front of the castle at least 45 minutes in advance. For the best view, you will want to be near Casey's Corner on Main Street, U.S.A - or anywhere in the hub in front of the castle. Get too close though, and you miss the fireworks behind the castle and cannot appreciate the projections.

The show can also be viewed from anywhere along Main Street, the Railroad Station at the park entrance, as well as from nearby hotels. You can also view the show from almost anywhere in the park but a key part of this show is the

projections, so a view of the front of the castle is ideal.

Halloween-themed fireworks play during Disney's Halloween Season parties, and during the Christmas parties, you can enjoy festive fireworks. On the 3rd and 4th July, you can enjoy Disney's Celebrate America! – A Fourth of July Concert in the Sky fireworks.

**Fireworks Dessert Party**
At Tomorrowland Terrace Restaurant, tempting desserts, fruits, and cheeses await. As showtime nears, Cast Members escort you to a prime standing area in the Plaza Garden for viewing of the nighttime fireworks spectacular. Then, watch as the skies ignite and Cinderella Castle glows.

The Fireworks Dessert Party is $99 for adults and $59 for children, tax included.

**Ferrytale Fireworks – A Sparkling Dessert Cruise**
Sail on an iconic, double-stack ferryboat with delectable desserts inspired by the landmarks around you, as well as a fabulous fruit and cheese spread.

Enjoy this sweet ending to your day, before watching the fireworks. The show audio is piped through the boat's sound system for this magical viewing.

This experience is offered on select dates and costs $99 for adults and $69 for ages 3 to 9, including tax and gratuity.

✿ **COVID-19 CHANGES:** A quick reminder that at the time of writing, all parades, live entertainment & fireworks are suspended. A new firework show is rumored to debut in 2021.

# EPCOT

EPCOT was the second theme park to open at Walt Disney World, in 1982. Its name is an acronym of 'Experimental Prototype Community of Tomorrow', Walt Disney's vision for the future of cities.

Although EPCOT never become a city of tomorrow, today's version of EPCOT is still one of the most unique theme park concepts anywhere in the world.

The park is split into two halves:
- *Future World* is where world-class attractions take you into the future and beyond. Here you can soar around the world on a paraglider, enter a futuristic test track and blast off into space.
- *World Showcase* is made up of Pavilions representing different countries. Here you are immersed in different cultures with food, attractions, architecture, and more. Each person working at the pavilions has actually been recruited to work there for a year by Disney from their own country for an extra layer of authenticity.

## ☼ COVID-19 CHANGES:

At the moment as well as needing a park ticket, you also **need a Park Pass Reservation** for the first park you wish to visit each day - do this at DisneyWorld.com. **Face coverings are required** for guests ages 2 and up at all times at the parks except when eating while stationary.

**Guests will be temperature screened** to enter the park. At the time of writing **all parades, shows and fireworks are suspended. FastPass+ and Single Rider lines are suspended at all parks.** International Cast Members are not staffing the World Showcase pavilions. Other offerings may be reduced or suspended.

# Future World

## Spaceship Earth

Inside the giant geodesic sphere (or the golf ball as most guests call it), there is a ride taking you on a slow-moving journey from the dawn of time to the internet age. It is a fun and fascinating tale that is worth experiencing.

Towards the end, there is even a fun interactive portion where you can design your own future on a touchscreen.

We recommend riding this attraction later in the day as many guests line up for it at park opening as it is located right at the entrance - due

| FP Yes | None | 📷 Yes | ✓ 13 mins | ⏳ Less than 30 mins |

to its nature, the ride never stops loading and unloading so lines constantly move.

In the afternoon and evenings, there is very unlikely to be any wait at all to get on the ride.

## Awesome Planet

This beautiful 10-minute show uses stunning visuals and in-theater effects such as wind and water to tell the story of planet Earth and why we must work to protect it.

## Walt Disney Imagineering Presents The EPCOT Experience

With EPCOT undergoing a multi-year transformation, this pavilion allows you to take a peek into the future of the theme park.

Inside using screens and projections onto a 3D EPCOT model you can

discover the upcoming changes to the park. These include the transformation of the park's icon - Spaceship Earth, a new Moana water walkthrough attraction, a Guardians of the Galaxy roller coaster with a

backward launch, the new HarmonioUS nighttime show, and *Remy's Ratatouille Adventure*.

The full presentation takes about 12 minutes but you can walk in and out as you wish.

## Guardians of the Galaxy: Mission Rewind [Expected 2021/22]

This will be one of the world's longest indoor roller coasters - apparently the storyline will be a big part of this coaster so we're expecting something similar to *Harry Potter and the*

*Escape from Gringotts* at Universal Orlando.

The ride cars will be able to spin to show you certain scenes and you can even expect a backward launch.

We have no more details for this ride at the moment, and the ride could open either in 2021 or 2022 due to COVID-19 construction delays.

# Test Track

A fun family thrill ride that takes you into the world of Chevrolet. In the queue line, you design your own vehicle on a touchscreen, which is then virtually tested against other riders' vehicles throughout the ride.

The ride itself is a fun exploration of how different factors can influence a car and its capability, efficiency, responsiveness, and power.

| | | | | | | |
|---|---|---|---|---|---|---|
|  Yes | 40" |  Yes | ⊘ | 5 mins | ⧖ | 60 to 120 mins |

This attraction is great fun but beware that the ride is intense. It is the fastest ride in all of the Walt Disney

World Resort and reaches speeds exceeding 60mph.

In the Single Rider line, waits rarely exceed 30 minutes.

# The Seas with Nemo and Friends

A slow-moving clam shell ride past one of the biggest aquariums in the world. Stare in to take a look at the fish, and look out for characters from Pixar's *Finding Nemo* woven into the ride storyline mixed in

| | | | | | | |
|---|---|---|---|---|---|---|
|  Yes | None |  No | ⊘ | 4 mins | ⧖ | Less than 20 mins |

the same tanks as real fish.

After riding, enjoy *Seabase* - a 5.7-million-liter aquarium with interactive exhibitions,

tutorials and glass panes to see straight into the water and observe its inhabitants.

# Living with the Land

A slow cruise with narration through greenhouses, fish farms, and more.

| | | | | | | |
|---|---|---|---|---|---|---|
|  Yes | None |  No | ⊘ | 14 mins | ⧖ | Less than 30 mins |

Learn about the land, how humans use it, and all it provides. Witness plant-growing technology

techniques such as hydroponics - where plants are grown in water without soil.

A "Behind the Seeds" paid walking tour is also available from the counter by *Soarin' Around the World*.

# Turtle Talk with Crush

| | | | | | | |
|---|---|---|---|---|---|---|
|  Yes | None |  No | ⊘ | 12 mins | ⧖ | Less than 20 mins |

A "totally cool" show with Finding Nemo's turtle Crush! This interactive show gets adults and kids alike to speak to Crush and ask him questions about the turtle world; meanwhile, Crush has some questions for you about the human world.

It is a whole lot of fun if you are willing to get involved. You might even learn to speak whale!

As well as characters from "Finding Nemo", others from "Finding Dory" make appearances.

# Mission: SPACE

Soar into space as you are put into an astronaut's shoes at EPCOT.

Disney offers two versions of this ride. The "less intense" green version is still reasonably intense as simulators go. The "more intense" orange version spins rapidly to push and pull you from your seat for a more intense experience. This creates the feeling of zero gravity but is more likely to make you nauseous.

We suggest not eating before riding this attraction or at least allow a few hours

| FP | Yes | 📏 44" | 📷 No | ⊘ 6 mins | ⧗ 20 to 60 mins |

to digest your food, as this ride is known for inducing motion sickness.

The post-ride area is the *Advanced Training Lab*. This is a digital indoor play area (including chargers in the seats).

# Journey into Imagination with Figment

This is perhaps the strangest attraction in all of Walt Disney World.

Your friend Figment (a purple dragon) wants to test out all five of your senses in this unusual slow-moving ride. It is a bizarre

| FP | Yes | 📏 N/A | 📷 No | ⊘ 8 mins | ⧗ Less than 10 mins |

experience that is worth doing at least once.

The post-ride area is called *ImageWorks*, and is a variety of fun interactive

games.

The post-ride area can also be entered via the shop if you do not wish to ride the attraction.

# Soarin' Around the World

One of EPCOT's most popular attractions, *Soarin'* gives you the chance to experience what it is like to fly and hang glide over places around the world.

It is a truly immersive experience with smells and

| FP | Yes | 📏 40" | 📷 No | ⊘ 5 mins | ⧗ 60 to 90 mins |

slow movement to match a giant on-screen video, creating an incredibly realistic sensation of flight. If you are scared of heights this ride is not for you.

This is truly one of the best attractions in the whole park - the concept is simple but the execution is excellent.

---

## DINING

**Coral Reef Restaurant** - Table Service, DDP accepted, entrées are $24-$40.
**Garden Grill Restaurant** - Table Service, No DDP, family-style with characters, breakfast is $27 for kids and $42 for adults, lunch & dinner is $36 for kids and $55 for adults.
**Space 220 (Opening 2021)** - Table Service. American cuisine with a view from space.
**Sunshine Seasons** - Snacks and Quick Service, DDP accepted, entrées are $9-$14.
**Taste Track Burgers and Fries** - Snacks and Quick Service, DDP accepted, prices vary seasonally.

# World Showcase

*The World Showcase is the second half of EPCOT. It is split into eleven countries' pavilions around a central lagoon. The World Showcase is your opportunity to explore different corners of the world, all just a stroll away from each other.*

Explore World Showcase's pavilions and move from Canada to the UK in just a few steps, or travel to China or Japan and discover new cultures. Shop, dine, experience attractions, and speak to representatives.

**Note**: Except for some food stands and dining locations, World Showcase and its attractions open at 11:00am, and not at 9:00am with Future World. The exceptions are the Norway and Mexico pavilions that open at 9:00am.

If you are staying at the EPCOT area hotels or arriving on Disney's Skyliner, you may use the park's International Gateway entrance from park opening, and walk from World Showcase to Future World.

**World Showcase Activities**:
• Disney Phineas and Ferb: EPCOT's World Showcase Adventure - Join Phineas and Ferb by becoming a special agent and exploring the countries' pavilions while completing missions

on a specially designed cell phone. This is great for entertaining kids who might otherwise find the World Showcase area a bit boring. This game is set to be replaced by a similar DuckTales game in 2021.
• Kidcot Fun Stops - Designed for the young kids, each country around the World Showcase features these "fun stops" with a variety of activities as you make your way around the World Showcase.

## Mexico

### Gran Fiesta Tour Starring The Three Caballeros

A slow-moving boat ride through classic Mexican landscapes. While you are admiring the scenery, José Carioca and Panchito (two of the Three Caballeros) are on the lookout for Donald Duck. This is a gentle adventure that rarely has a wait. We recommend this cruise if you fancy a relaxing ride that is family-friendly - plus there is some fun lively music. It is a bit like *"it's a small world"* but just for Mexico.

| FP | No | | None | 📷 | No | ⌄ | 8 mins | ⧖ | Less than 10 mins |
|----|----|----|------|----|----|----|--------|----|-------|

### Mexico Folk Art Gallery

This gallery features temporary exhibitions about Mexico and its culture.

---

**DINING**

**Choza de Margarita** - Bar, No DDP, drinks are $6-$15.50, small dishes are $4.50-$15
**La Cava del Tequila** - Bar, No DDP, drinks are $14-$21
**La Cantina de San Angel** - Quick Service, DDP accepted, entrées are $9.50-$14.50.
**La Hacienda de San Angel** - Table Service, DDP accepted, dinner only, entrées are $21-$36
**San Angel Inn Restaurante** - Table Service, DDP accepted, entrées are $18-$38

# Norway

## Frozen Ever After

This attraction is an incredible adventure fit for the entire family with some of the most incredible animatronics and technology ever seen on a Disney attraction.

Guests are transported to the 'Winter in Summer Celebration', visit Elsa's Ice Palace and the North Mountain, along with other locations, before returning to the Bay of Arendelle. A photo is taken of guests wearing a MagicBand.

This is an absolute must-do

| FP | Yes | | None | 📷 | Yes | ✓ | 5 mins | ⏳ | 60 to 90 mins |
|----|-----|--|------|----|-----|---|--------|----|----|

attraction. Minimize waits by getting here when the park opens, or reserve FastPass+ well in advance.

## Plus...

**Royal Summerhus** - A well-themed and fun meet-and-greet with Frozen's Anna and Elsa.

**Stave Church Gallery** - This gallery showcases Norwegian artifacts. Many of these details inspired the writers behind the hit Disney movie 'Frozen'. Exhibitions change periodically.

> ### DINING
> **Akershus Royal Banquet Hall** - Buffet with Characters, DDP accepted, breakfast is $53 per adult and $34 per child, lunch & dinner is $63 per adult and $41 for kids.
> **Kringla Bakeri Og Kafe** - Snacks and Quick Service, DDP accepted, entrées are $8-$10

# China

## Wondrous China (Opening 2021)

'Wondrous China' is a 360-degree movie inspiring you to visit this fascinating country. Along the journey, you can expect to see landmarks such as The Great Wall of China. This show is standing room only.

## House of the Whispering Willows

This walk-through attraction features temporary exhibitions about China. At the time of writing, the exhibition is about Disney's newest resort, Shanghai Disneyland.

> ### DINING
> **Joy of Tea** - Snacks, DDP accepted, serves drinks, desserts, and snacks, snacks are $4-$11
> **Lotus Blossom Café** - Quick Service, DDP accepted, entrées are $10-$11
> **Nine Dragons Restaurant** - Table Service, DDP accepted, entrées are $16-$25 at lunch and $16-$34 at dinner

# Germany

*This pavilion only has a small outdoor area but contains the huge Biergarten restaurant. There are stores here, but there are no attractions.*

## DINING

**Biergarten Restaurant -** Buffet, DDP accepted, adult meals are $46 and children's are $29 at lunch and dinner
**Sommerfest -** Snacks and Quick Service, DDP accepted, sausages are $10.

# Italy

*Enjoy the photo opportunities, dine, and shop. There are no attractions here.*

## DINING

**Gelati -** Snacks, No DDP, ice creams are $7-$11.
**Tutto Gusto Wine Cellar** - Bar, No DDP, small dishes: $12-$26, entrees are $16-$32.
**Tutto Italia Ristorante -** Table Service, DDP accepted, entrées are $19-$36 at lunch & dinner.
**Via Napoli Ristorante e Pizzeria** - Table Service, DDP, individual pizzas start at $23, and family-size pizzas are up to $49.

# Japan

The Japan pavilion is one of our favorites. It is serene, filled with beautiful photo opportunities, and you really do feel transported away from a busy theme park. Part of the reason for this is that there is no major attraction here. Instead, the majority of the pavilion is a huge shop that sells everything Japanese, from food to lampshades, and pearls to comic books.

The **Bijutsu-kan Gallery** features exhibits on Japanese history, which change regularly.

## DINING

**Kabuki Café -** Snacks, No DDP, snacks and sushi are $5-$9.
**Katsura Grill -** Quick Service, DDP accepted, entrées are $9-$14.
**Takumi-Tei -** Signature Table Service, No DDP, entrees are $40-$120. A 9-course tasting menu is $180. Dinner only.
**Teppan Edo -** Table Service, DDP accepted, entrées are $24-$37.
**Tokyo Dining -** Table Service, DDP accepted, entrées are $21-$36.

# The American Adventure

## The American Adventure

Before watching this show, explore the inside of the pavilion building for paintings and quotes from historical American figures. Get to the building well before showtime to enjoy the "Voices of Liberty" a cappella choir who sings patriotic songs, as well as Disney classics.
The show retells the U.S.A.'s history. It is educational and well-paced, but won't thrill.

| | | | | | |
|---|---|---|---|---|---|
| No | None | No | 28 mins | At set times |

## American Heritage Gallery

This gallery features temporary exhibits covering American history.

> **DINING**
> **Fife & Drum Tavern** - Snacks, DDP accepted, drinks are $4-$14, snacks are $5-$13.
> **Regal Eagle Smokehouse Inn** - Quick Service, DDP accepted, entrées are $11.50-$19

# Morocco

*The Morocco pavilion is absolutely stunning and immediately stands out as one of the most authentic-looking pavilions. From the small passageways to the marketplace area with street sellers, it all feels very real.*

## Gallery of Arts and History

This gallery features temporary exhibits covering Moroccan history.

> **DINING**
> **Restaurant Marrakesh** - Table Service, DDP accepted, entrées are $22-$36, or $55 for a 3-course set meal
> **Spice Road Table** - Table Service, DDP accepted, small plates are $9-$13, entrées: $25-$35
> **Tangierine Café** - Quick Service, DDP accepted, entrées are $11-$17

# Canada

## Canada Far and Wide

 No  None  No  13 minutes  Until next show

Explore the wonder of the breadth of this beautiful country from the beautiful mountains to the dynamic cities. This show is standing room only as it is presented in 360-degree circle-vision.

> **Dining**
> **Le Cellier Steakhouse** - Table Service, DDP accepted – 2 Table Service credits, entrées: $34-$57

# France

## Remy's Ratatouille Adventure (Opening 2021)

Due to open in 2021, *Ratatouille* is a trackless dark ride for the whole family. Here you board a 'ratmobile' and travel through Paris' streets, rooftops, and kitchens in a 4D immersive ride featuring giant video screens, scents, water effects, and much more.

When it opens, this ride will be the newest in the park and therefore it will get the longest waits - expect waits of over two hours pretty much daily.

The ride will offer FastPass+ and a Single Rider line (although these are suspended during COVID-19).

## Impressions de France / Beauty and the Beast Sing-Along

This theater showcases two shows - currently, this is *Impressions* until 7pm, and Beauty and the Beast after. Explore France through a cinematic video on five screens spanning 220 degrees with well-known landmarks, and hidden gems in Impressions de France. Alternatively, sing along to Beauty and the Beast songs.

No | None | No | 14 mins | Until next show

### DINING

**Chefs de France** - Table Service, DDP accepted, entrées are $22-$37
**Monsieur Paul** - Signature Table Service Restaurant (2 credits required), DDP accepted, dinner only, entrées are $41-$47. There are also 3-course set menus at $89 and $119.
**La Creperie de Paris (Opens 2021)** - Table Service and Quick Service.
**L'Artisan des Glaces** - Snacks, No DDP, ice creams are $5-$12
**Les Halles Boulangerie & Patisserie** - Snacks, DDP accepted, items are $3-$11.

# United Kingdom

*Themed to a quaint English town, there is always a lot going on here, from the pub's atmosphere to the meet-and-greets to stage performances.*

*There are, of course, many shops to explore. There are no attractions at the UK pavilion.*

### DINING

**Rose & Crown Pub & Dining Room** - Table Service, DDP accepted, entrées are $21-$27
**Yorkshire County Fish Shop** - Quick Service, DDP accepted, meals are $11.50
**UK Beer Cart** - Drinks location, No DDP, alcoholic beverages are $10-$11

# More about EPCOT

## Transportation – World Showcase Boats

The full walk around the World Showcase Lagoon (without exploring any of the countries) loop is 1.2 miles, but if you want to get across from one side to another quickly, catch one of the boats. Boats depart from the Future World side of the lagoon and go across to the Germany and Morocco pavilions.

## World Showcase Entrance

EPCOT's main entrance is by *Spaceship Earth* leading to Future World, but the park also has a "back" entrance leading to the World Showcase located by the UK and French pavilions. It is most often used by those staying at the Boardwalk, Yacht and Beach Club, and Swan and Dolphin resorts, although anyone may use it. Boats to Disney's Hollywood Studios are by this entrance. Skyliner guests also arrive at this entrance.

# EPCOT Live Entertainment

**JAMMitors (Future World)** – Janitors use their tools to make music.

**Mariachi Cobre (Mexican pavilion)** – A Mexican folk band.

**Sahara Beat (Moroccan pavilion)** – Dance and sing to the rhythms of Morocco.

**Jeweled Dragon Acrobats (Chinese pavilion)** – This acrobatic troupe performs stunts.

**Sergio (Italian pavilion)** – A football juggler.

**Voices of Liberty (American Adventure pavilion)** –

Incredible voices, and songs from throughout U.S. history, as well as Disney songs.

**Matsuriza (Japanese pavilion)** – Traditional Taiko drumming.

**Serveur Amusant (French pavilion)** – French acrobats dazzle with incredible skills.

**Rose & Crown Pub Musician (UK pavilion)** – Live music every evening.

**Bodh'aktan (Canadian Pavilion)** – Music that combines Celtic, Trad-Quebecois, Polka, Punk, Irish Folk, Breton, and Maritime.

**Groovin' Alps (German Pavilion)** – A high-energy German percussion band who brings the sounds of the mountains to EPCOT with folk tunes played on items found on a farm.

**COVID-19 Reminder**: All live entertainment is suspended.

# Nighttime Spectacular: HarmonioUS

2021 brings EPCOT a new nighttime spectacular - *HarmonioUS*.
Disney says: "This new show will celebrate how Disney music inspires people around the world, and will feature massive floating set pieces, custom-built LED panels, choreographed moving fountains, lights, pyrotechnics and lasers."

# Disney's Hollywood Studios

Spanning 135 acres, Disney's Hollywood Studios was the third theme park to be built at the Walt Disney World Resort and opened in 1989. The park is themed around Hollywood in the 1930s and 1940s. It hosted over 11.4 million guests in 2019, making it the ninth most visited theme park in the world, but the least visited park at the Walt Disney World Resort.

## Live Entertainment

### Fantasmic – Nighttime Spectacular

| | | | | | |
|---|---|---|---|---|---|
| 🎟 Yes | None | 📷 No | ⌄ | 30 mins | ⏳ At set times |

*Fantasmic* is Disney's Hollywood Studios' nighttime spectacular. The show combines character performances, water screen projections, fireworks, lasers, pyrotechnics and more. It should not be missed and appeals to all ages.

Arrive early to get the best seats in the 11,000-seat outdoor arena. If there are two performances on the same night, crowds will be smaller at the second one. The Fastpass+ seating area takes up about half of the stadium-style seating, so be sure to arrive early even with a Fastpass+ reservation as there is no guarantee of a great view.

Certain dining packages entitle you to reserved seating.

At off-peak times, 'Fantasmic' only runs on select nights.

⚙ **COVID-19 CHANGES:**
At the moment as well as needing a park ticket, you also **need a Park Pass Reservation** for the first park you wish to visit each day - do this at DisneyWorld.com. **Face coverings are required** for guests ages 2 and up at all times at the parks except when eating while stationary. **Guests will be temperature screened** to enter the park. At the time of writing **all parades, shows and fireworks are suspended. FastPass+ and Single Rider lines are suspended at all parks.** Other offerings may be reduced or suspended.

# Hollywood Boulevard

*Recreated to be like Hollywood with shops and restaurants, Hollywood Boulevard is the theme park equivalent of Main Street, U.S.A. in Magic Kingdom Park. It is the park's opening scene.*

## Mickey & Minnie's Runaway Railway

*Mickey & Minnie's Runaway Railway* is the newest attraction at Disney's Hollywood Studios, having opened in March 2020.

The fun begins when you see the premiere of a new cartoon short with Mickey and Minnie getting ready for a picnic.

As they head out, they drive alongside a train and see that the engineer is Goofy. Then, one magical moment lets you step into the movie and on Goofy's train for a wacky, wild ride.

FP Yes | None | 📷 No | ⌄ 5 mins | ⧗ 60 to 90 mins

*Mickey & Minnie's Runaway Railway* puts you inside the wacky and unpredictable world of a Mickey Mouse Cartoon Short where you're the star and anything can happen. It's a fun family-friendly ride.

---

### DINING

**The Hollywood Brown Derby** - Table Service, DDP accepted, entrées are $18-$49. Lounge drinks are $14-$17. Small plates are $11-$20.
**The Trolley Car Café** - Starbucks location serving drinks and snacks, DDP accepted, drinks and snacks are $4-$6 each.

# Sunset Boulevard

## The Twilight Zone: Tower of Terror

*Tower of Terror* transports you to another dimension dropping you 199 feet straight down.

The atmosphere is truly immersive and contains some of the best theming at Walt Disney World. The on-ride effects before the actual drops are great, and it really does feel like your elevator is out of control. The drops are fun but scary. The adrenaline is incredible, and it is definitely worth the visit.

| FP | Yes | 📏 40" | 📷 Yes | ✓ | ⏱ 2 mins | ⌛ 20 to 60 mins |

Motors pull the elevator down faster than gravity, creating a weightless feeling. The ride has different drops each time.

## Rock 'n' Roller Coaster: Starring Aerosmith

*Rock 'n' Roller Coaster* is a high-speed indoor roller coaster. Hop aboard a Limo and take a high-speed ride through the Hollywood hills.

You will go through 4.5Gs and reach speeds of 60mph in 3 seconds.

| FP | Yes | 📏 48" | 📷 Yes | ✓ | ⏱ 5 mins | ⌛ 40 to 85 mins |

Each Limo is equipped with speakers around your body for ultimate enjoyment.

There are inversions and loops. If you are not a roller coaster fan, then this ride is not for you.

A Single Rider line is available.

## Beauty and the Beast - Live on Stage

Step into the world of Belle and Gaston for a whirlwind version of the Disney classic 'Beauty and the Beast'. This show is just like stepping into a Broadway performance with fantastic sets, costumes, and props. It is well worth a viewing.

## Lightning McQueen's Racing Academy

See a full-size Lightning McQueen show you his latest racing simulator in this fun 12-minute show. It is a good place to take a break with minimal waits, and great fun for Cars fans.

---

### DINING

**Anaheim Produce** - Snacks, No DDP, pretzels and churros are $6-$7. Serves drinks.
**Catalina Eddie's** - Quick Service, DDP accepted, entrées (pizza and salads) are $8-$11
**Fairfax Fare** - Quick Service, DDP accepted, entrées are $8-$13.50
**Hollywood Scoops** - Snacks, No DDP, ice creams are $5.50-$7
**Rosie's All-American Café** - Quick Service, DDP accepted, entrées $10-$13.50
**Sunshine Day Bar** - Quick Service, DDP accepted, drinks are $4-$14

---

# Animation Courtyard

*A good mixture of shows and walkthroughs await you in this area of the park.*

## Voyage of The Little Mermaid

 Yes |  None |  No | ⊘ 15 mins | ⧖ At set times

This show is a mixture of live actors, puppets, and light, laser, and rain effects retelling the story of The Little Mermaid.

**Warning:** The large Ursula puppet used during the show may scare some younger children.

## Star Wars Launch Bay

This is a walkthrough exhibit featuring meet-and-greets with Star Wars characters, props from the movies, and games to play.

It is a haven for Star Wars fans.

## Disney Junior Dance Party

 Yes | ⊘ Unknown

With catchy songs, puppets and a toddler-friendly environment, Disney Junior Dance Party is designed for the younger members of the family.

This live show experience takes its inspiration from popular Disney Junior shows on TV, including "Mickey and the Roadster Racers," "Doc McStuffins," "The Lion Guard" and "Vampirina."

## Walt Disney Presents

🎫 No | 📏 None | 📷 No | ⊘ 10-30 mins | ⧖ None

This walkthrough exhibit details the fascinating life of Walt Disney, from his humble beginnings to his vision for Walt Disney World years later.

As you move along the timeline, you can read the information, watch videos, and see models of the original Disneyland.

You can even see the newest additions to Disney theme parks around the world. It is a fascinating insight for aspiring Imagineers.

At the end of the exhibition, you can either exit or you can watch an 18-minute short movie retelling Walt Disney's life story - all narrated by the man himself.

The theater is often used to show extended movie previews for upcoming Disney and Pixar productions. If this is the case during your visit, the movie preview will replace the movie about Walt Disney.

# Echo Lake

## Star Tours - The Adventures Continue

Enter an intergalactic spaceport with StarSpeeders, an alien air traffic control station, and robots hard at work to make your journey unforgettable.

Board your vehicle for a tour of one of many planets – each time, the ride is slightly different, with over 50 different scene combinations!

If you are prone to motion sickness, *Star Tours* should be avoided as this is a

| | Yes | 40" | No | 5 mins | 15 to 45 mins |

motion simulator. If you want a milder ride, ask for the front row as the movements are less jarring.

## Jedi Training – Trials of the Temple

For the younger adventurers, this is the chance to get up on stage and yield a lightsaber and battle the dark side.

Only children can participate in the

| | No | None | No | 15 mins | At set times |

experience. For those not participating, the show is still entertaining to watch.

Jedi Training takes place several times per day on the stage to the left of *Star Tours: The Adventures Continue*. Consult your park Times Guide for showtimes.

## Indiana Jones Epic Stunt Spectacular

See Indi and his friends take on some death-defying stunts. Get ready for set changes, audience

| | Yes | None | No | 30 mins | At set times |

interaction, and an explosive finale. A definite must-watch for any day in the Studios.

## For the First Time in Forever: A "Frozen" Celebration

Watch a retelling of the "Frozen" story with the historians of Arendelle. As the story evolves, the show becomes a sing-a-long every

| | Yes | None | No | 25 mins | At set times |

time a song comes on. The show culminates with the arrival of Anna and Elsa, making for a stunning finale.

---

### DINING

**50's Prime Time Café** - Table Service, DDP accepted, entrées are $17-$28
**Backlot Express** - Snacks and Quick Service, DDP accepted, entrées are $9-$14
**Dockside Diner** - Quick Service, DDP accepted, entrées are $11-$13
**Epic Eats** - Snacks, no DDP, desserts are $5.50-$8.50, drinks are $3.50-$14
**Hollywood & Vine** - Buffet Service, DDP accepted, breakfast is $42 per adult & $27 per child, lunch is $55 for adults & $36.
**Tune-In Lounge** - Bar, No DDP, drinks are $8 and upwards.

# Commissary Lane & Grand Av.

## Muppet Vision 3D

For Muppets fans, this is one attraction that should not be missed - a 3D experience with in-theater special effects, live-action and more.

 Yes | None  No | 30 mins | 15 mins or less

This attraction is a good one to save for when you need a break from the heat, rain or walking, and often has low wait times.

Be prepared for a long, pre-show before the main 3D movie, which is very enjoyable. The show time listed includes the pre-show.

### DINING

**ABC Commissary** - Quick Service and Snacks, DDP accepted, entrées are $10-$18
**Baseline Tap House** - Lounge, No DDP, small plates $6-$11, also serves drinks
**Sci-Fi Dine-In Theater Restaurant** - Table Service, DDP accepted, entrées are $17-$33
**Mama Melrose's Ristorante Italiano** - Table Service, DDP accepted, entrées are $19-$33
**Pizzerizzo** - Quick Service, DDP accepted, entrées are $10-$11. Open seasonally.

# Toy Story Land

## Toy Story Mania

One of Walt Disney World's most popular attractions, *Toy Story Mania* draws huge crowds of all ages; the result is long waits.

The ride is an interactive virtual shooting experience

 Yes | None No | 5 mins | 45 to 75 mins

where each passenger in the car is given a gun to shoot at interactive screens with Toy Story characters. In some scenes, you will shoot

plates, in other balloons, with the aim to get the most points.

## Slinky Dog Dash

Slinky Dog invites you aboard his small but mighty family-friendly coaster.

Get great views of the surrounding area as you

 Yes | 38"  Yes | 90 secs | 60 to 90 mins

whiz across Toy Story Land on the Mega Coaster Play Kit that Andy's assembled.

This is a good starter coaster for kids - we recommend a FastPass+ reservation to ease the wait.

## Alien Swirling Saucers

Hop inside a flying saucer powered by the Green Aliens from the Toy Story movies.

You will spin on a wild ride into space as you whip

Yes | 32" No | 90 secs | 40 to 60 mins

round each corner.

This attraction is very similar to the tea cups at Magic

Kingdom but with bigger forces as you change direction. Fun for (almost) the whole family.

### DINING

**Woody's Lunch Box** - Quick Service, DDP accepted, entrées are $6-$9 at breakfast and $9-$13 at lunch and dinner.
**Woody's Roundup BBQ** - Table Service. Opening in 2021.

# Star Wars: Galaxy's Edge

## Star Wars: Rise of the Resistance

*Rise of the Resistance* may be Disney's most incredible ride ever - it is part-simulator, park-dark ride, and part-show.

At the time of writing, the ride does not offer either a standby line or FastPass+ reservations. To ride, you must use the My Disney Experience app to get a Boarding Group on the day of your visit at exactly 7:00am - you do not need to be inside the park (so can

| 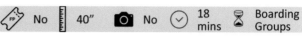 No | 40" | 📷 No | ✓ 18 mins | ⏳ Boarding Groups |

do it from your hotel room for example) but you must have a confirmed ticket and Park Pass Reservation. You will need to be very quick as boarding groups for the whole day disappear in seconds - those with the fastest-fingers get to ride, those who are too slow, miss out. Each person in your party should try on their phones to increase

your chance of success - we recommend you begin refreshing at 6:59am.

If successful, Disney will send an app notification to when it is your turn to ride - you won't be given a specific time slot in advance.

The 18-minute ride time includes several pre-shows.

## Millennium Falcon: Smugglers Run

*Smugglers Run* is an interactive simulator, which is a bit like an upgraded version of *Star Tours*.

In the queue, each guest is assigned a role for their flight - either a pilot, gunner, or engineer. Then, when you

| Yes | 38" | 📷 No | ✓ 5 mins | ⏳ 30 to 60 mins |

board your 6-seater vehicle be sure to stay alert to hear what you'll need to do to steer your ship to safety.

Unlike, a normal simulator,

here your actions have consequences so if you crash the Millennium Falcon, you'll know! A Single Rider line is available (but suspended due to COVID).

---

As well as an incredibly-detailed area with lots of shopping, dining, and the two main attractions above, you may enjoy the following experiences available at an extra charge:
- **Savi's Workshop - Handbuilt Lightsabers** - In this 20-minute experience, you get to build a lightsaber from scratch. These lightsabers are much-better quality items than the normal ones and are not really toys but display pieces, and they should be - this workshop costs $200, plus tax. Reservations are recommended.
- **Droid Depot** - You build either a BB-style or R-style remote-controlled droid. You choose your parts from a conveyor belt, build your droid, and then activate it. The whole experience takes about 20 minutes. You are given a carry box for your droid but may not play with the droid on the ground inside the park. The droid will interact with the different areas of Galaxy's Edge through various beeps, lights and movements and will react when it sees other droids. The droid experience is $100 - to add a backpack is an additional $50.

---

## DINING

**Kat Saka's Kettle** - Snacks. DDP accepted. Sells popcorn ($6.50), orb soda ($5.50) & water.
**Ronto Roasters** - Quick Service. DDP accepted. Serves oats ($7), wraps ($12.50) and snack samplers ($20). Also serves alcoholic ($13-$15) beverages, as well as hot and cold drinks.
**Docking Bay 7 Food and Cargo** - Quick Service. DDP accepted. Serves breakfast. Lunch and dinner entrees include pot roast, pork ribs and chicken salad ($14-$19).
**Oga's Cantina** - Bar/Lounge. No DDP. Serves non-alcoholic ($7-$13) and alcoholic drinks ($17-$45) including Blue Milk, plus snacks.
**Milk Stand** - Snack Kiosk. DDP accepted. Serves snacks and Blue and Green milk as a non-alcoholic ($8) or alcoholic drink ($14).

# Disney's Animal Kingdom Park

Disney's Animal Kingdom Park is Walt Disney World's fourth and newest theme park; it opened in 1998. Spanning 580 acres, it is the largest Disney park ever built. It is so big that you could fit all the other theme parks at Walt Disney World inside it and have room to spare.

Animal Kingdom is the best themed of all the parks with remarkable attention to detail. This is the sixth most visited park in the world, with 13.9 million visitors in 2019.

The entrance area of the park is called Oasis. It is a forest-like setting with winding pathways and a relaxing feel. The **Oasis Exhibits** are home to exotic animals. For those wanting to eat in this area, there is Rainforest Café (Table Service, DDP accepted, entrées are $9-$16 at breakfast, and $17-$37 at lunch and dinner).

## Live Shows

### Festival of the Lion King

'Festival of The Lion King' is our favorite show at Walt Disney World and a true celebration of the essence of The Lion King movies. The show does not follow a movie storyline, but instead includes the best songs interpreted by professionals in an African-inspired theme. This is a definite must-do. This show is presented in the Africa area of the park.

### Finding Nemo: The Musical

This is a Broadway-style show that has convinced us that Finding Nemo should have been a musical all along! The show has great sets, costumes and actors. Take the time to see this family-friendly production. This show is located in the Dinoland USA area of the park.

### Rivers of Light - Nighttime Spectacular

This nighttime spectacular features live music, floating lanterns, water screens and swirling animal imagery bringing a show to Discovery River that delights guests and truly caps off their day. Dedicated viewing and seating areas are available in Asia and Dinoland USA.

☼ **COVID-19 CHANGES:**
At the moment as well as needing a park ticket, you also **need a Park Pass Reservation** for the first park you wish to visit each day - do this at DisneyWorld.com. **Face coverings are required** for guests ages 2 and up at all times at the parks except when eating while stationary. **Guests will be temperature screened** to enter the park. At the time of writing **all parades, shows and fireworks are suspended**. **FastPass+ and Single Rider lines are suspended at all parks.** Other offerings may be reduced or suspended.

# Discovery Island

*This is the hub area of the park that holds the astounding Tree of Life, and leads to all the other lands of the park.*

## Tree of Life

Discover over 320 animals carved into this 145-foot tree, as you walk around it. The attention to detail is amazing – a true masterpiece.

At the **Discovery Island Trails**, you can find otters, lemurs, flamingos, red kangaroos, storks, tortoises and more.

After sunset, stick around for the tree of life's "awakenings" throughout the evening.

## It's Tough to be a Bug

 Yes  None  No  9 mins  Less than 20 mins

The meanest and nastiest 3D show we have ever experienced. Be prepared to see how humans treat insects and then get a taste of your own medicine. Even when you think it is over, it is not! This attraction is likely to frighten adults and terrify children. We do not recommend making FastPass+ reservations as the queues for this show are usually very short.

## Adventurers Outpost Meet and Greet

 Yes  Less than 30 mins

Get a photo with Mickey and Minnie in their Safari gear at this location. This is often one of the least crowded meet and greets featuring Mickey at any of the four parks.

## Winged Encounters: The Kingdom Takes Flight

This show takes place in front of the Tree of Life. It features different types of macaw and gives guests a chance to see them up close.

**DINING**

**Creature Comforts** - Starbucks, DDP, drinks and snacks are $3-$6
**Eight Spoon Café** - Snacks, no DDP, individual snacks are $3-$7.
**Flame Tree Barbecue** - Snacks and Quick Service, DDP accepted, entrées are $11-$19
**Isle of Java** - Snacks, no DDP, pastries, pretzels and biscuits are $4-$7.
**Nomad Lounge** - Bar and lounge, No DDP, small plates are $9 to $18, drinks vary in price.
**Pizzafari** - Quick Service, DDP accepted, pizzas, salads and flatbreads are $10-$13.50
**Tiffins** - Signature Table Service, DDP accepted (2 Table Service credits), entrées are $30-$65.

# DinoLand U.S.A

*Themed to a traveling carnival, DinoLand has several attractions listed below. As well as these there are also the Fossil Fun Games (carnival-style games – extra charge to play) and The Boneyard (a play area) to explore.*

## DINOSAUR

This is a scary, loud and turbulent journey through the past as you venture in search of an iguanodon dinosaur.

However, things may not go quite to plan.

This ride is a great thrill with an incredible ride vehicle, great storytelling and an immersive storyline.

It is a fun blast into the past but will likely scare younger

| FP | Yes | 📏 40" | 📷 Yes | ✓ 3 mins | ⏳ 20 to 45 min |
|---|---|---|---|---|---|

visitors due to the darkness and the loud sound effects used throughout the attraction.

## TriceraTop Spin

| FP | No | 📏 None |
|---|---|---|
| 📷 | No | ✓ 90 secs |
| ⏳ | Less than 15 mins | |

This is a spinning ride just like Dumbo at the Magic Kingdom but themed to dinosaurs. It is fun, but nothing revolutionary, and usually has short queues.

You can control how your dinosaur's height with a lever. Great for younger kids.

## DINING
**Dino-Bite Snacks** - Snacks, No DDP, serves ice creams at $5.50-$8
**Dino Diner** - Snacks, No DDP, serves chip pies and hot/corn dogs at $8.50-$11
**Restaurantosaurus** - Quick Service, DDP accepted, entrées are $10-$17
**Trilo-Bites** - Snacks, No DDP, sells ice creams and shakes for $5-$6, and drinks

# Africa

*Travel to the African continent into a land filled with character and spice.*

## Kilimanjaro Safaris

Traverse the world's largest man-made savannah, spanning 110 acres on-board *Kilimanjaro Safaris*.

Join your guide for a ride on a safari-style truck and get closer to the animals than you ever thought possible at a theme park.

Make sure you bring your camera as you may just get to see hippos, giraffes, monkeys, zebras, lions and more on this unpredictable adventure. It really is different every single time. The queue line for this attraction is tedious, so we

| | | | | | |
|---|---|---|---|---|---|
| FP Yes | None | 📷 No | ⏱ 20 mins | ⏳ 30 to 60 min |

recommend you make a FastPass+ reservation if possible.

**Top Tip**: The animals are most active in the morning before it gets too hot, or straight after it rains.

## Gorilla Falls Exploration Trail

See gorillas, monkeys, meerkats, birds and more in this self-guided walkthrough attraction.

This is a relaxing change from the long waits of many of the major attractions at this park. Here you can take the animals in at your own pace.

## Wildlife Express Train

This is more a method of transport between Africa and Rafiki's Planet Watch than an actual attraction.

There are a few minor things to see along the way and it is a good place to rest for a few minutes or to seek shelter from the rain.

---

### DINING

**Dawa Bar** - Bar, No DDP, drinks are $9-$14

**Harambe Fruit Market** - Snacks, DDP accepted, the fruit is $2-$6

**Harambe Market** - Quick Service, DDP accepted, entrées are $10-$13.50

**Kusafiri Coffee Shop & Bakery** - Snacks and Quick service, No DDP, curries are $10.50-$11.50

**Tamu Tamu Refreshments** - Drinks and Desserts, No DDP, ice creams are $6-$7 and alcoholic drinks are $9-$11.

**Tusker House Restaurant** - Buffet, DDP accepted, character breakfast is $42 per adult and $27 per child. The non-character lunch and dinner buffet is $55 per adult, $36 per child.

# Rafiki's Planet Watch

*To get to Rafiki's Planet Watch you will need to catch the Wildlife Express Train from the Africa area of the Park.*

### Habitat Habit!

Learn about how to protect endangered cotton-top tamarins in their natural homes. Guests also learn how to create animal habitats in their own homes.

### Conservation Station

See the conservation efforts undertaken by The Walt Disney Company and take a behind the scenes look at how the animals are taken care of at Disney's Animal Kingdom, including a look at an examination room.

### Affection Section

This is essentially a petting zoo with domesticated animals. Sometimes Cast Members will be present to tell you facts about the animals here.

### "It All Started with a Mouse"

 No  20 mins

Conservation Station's "animal ambassadors" including sheep, parrots, porcupines, birds of prey and Kunekune pigs help tell stories and make appearances in, around, and even above the audience in this show.

Cast Members share natural history fun facts, conservation messages and inspiring calls-to-action.

After the show, you can meet some of the stars of the show and are encouraged to capture once-in-a-lifetime memories with plenty of photographs.

# Asia

### Expedition Everest - Legend of the Forbidden Mountain

*Expedition Everest* is an incredible ride through the Forbidden Mountain where you might just get to see The Yeti in his natural habitat! The queue line is incredible - you even pass through a yeti museum while waiting!

As well as the big drop outside the attraction, there are a few other surprises. The ride reaches speeds of 50mph. *Expedition Everest* is

| FP | Yes | 📏 44" | 📷 Yes | ✓ | ⌛ 3 mins | ⏳ 30 to 70 min |

great fun and this is one of Disney's best-ever rides!

## Maharajah Jungle Trek

Take this self-guided walk and see komodo dragons, fruit bats, pythons, Bengal tigers, birds, deer, water buffalo and more. This is an absolute must-visit for animal fans and it is the most exciting and interesting of the trails in our opinion, although this will depend on which animals you prefer to see.

## Kali River Rapids

This fun raft water ride takes you through the forest. Everyone will be at least a little bit wet - but one or two people will usually get soaked.

This attraction is particularly

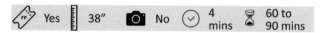

| FP | Yes | 📏 38" | 📷 No | ✓ | ⌛ 4 mins | ⏳ 60 to 90 mins |

popular on hot summer days. We recommend making a FastPass+ reservation as the queue line is slow.

There are free lockers outside the ride entrance for storing belongings.

## UP! A Great Bird Adventure

This 25-minute bird show is unlike any other with a fun storyline, a range of birds and some pretty impressive tricks, as well as Doug and Russell from the hit-movie 'Up!'. The seating area is covered, providing shade and shelter, but it is not air-conditioned. This show is presented up to 5 times daily in the Asia area of the park.

---

### DINING

**Anandapur Ice Cream Truck** - Snacks, no DDP, ice creams are $5-$5.50.

**Drinkwallah** - Snacks and drinks, drinks are $3.50-$5.50, chips and nut snacks are $3-$6.

**Mr. Kamal's** - Snacks, DDP accepted, dumplings, hummus and fries are $5-$6 each.

**Thirsty River Bar and Trek Snacks** - Bar and Snacks, No DDP, snacks are $3-$7

**Warung Outpost** - Snacks, No DDP, sells pretzels ($7), chips ($3) and drinks incl. alcohol

**Yak & Yeti Local Food Cafes** - Quick Service, DDP accepted, entrées are $9-$12 at breakfast and $12-$15 at lunch and dinner

**Yak & Yeti Quality Beverages Lounge** - Bar, No DDP, entrées are $12-$16, drinks: $4-$11

**Yak & Yeti Restaurant** - Table Service, DDP accepted, small plates, entrées are $19-$32

---

# Pandora: World of Avatar

*Inspired by the highest-grossing film of all time, Pandora: World of Avatar is Animal Kingdom's newest area. It opened in Summer 2017,*

## AVATAR: Flight of Passage

*Flight of Passage* is Animal Kingdom's most popular attraction, and one of the most technologically advanced attractions Disney has ever created.

This motion simulator has you sitting on the back of a Banshee (flying creature) and then soaring around the world of Pandora - around mountains, water, and scenery.

| | | | | | | | | |
|---|---|---|---|---|---|---|---|---|
| FP | Yes | | 44" | 📷 | No | ✓ | 4.5 mins | ⏳ 120 to 180 mins |

Through the 3D goggles, high-definition video and all sorts of clever sensory techniques, you are transported to another world - this is an immersive experience not to miss.

Guests who are scared of heights or simulated drops may wish to avoid this ride.

The ride vehicles are individual motorbike-style restraints and may not accommodate larger guests.

Expect long wait times throughout the whole day - head here as soon as the park opens if you don't manage to get a FastPass+ reservation. On the busiest of days, expect to see a wait of up to 4 hours.

## Na'vi River Journey

*Na'vi River Journey* is Pandora's more family-friendly attraction. Here you sit on a riverboat and calmly pass the nighttime jungle scenery of Pandora.

You'll see creatures, bioluminescent plants and other forest life around you.

The most impressive part of the ride is when you see a shaman beating musical drums - this is an incredibly lifelike animatronic

| | | | | | | | | |
|---|---|---|---|---|---|---|---|---|
| FP | Yes | | None | 📷 | No | ✓ | 4.5 mins | ⏳ 60 to 90 mins |

(pictured) that has to be seen to be believed.

There are no moments that should frighten children.

---

### DINING

**Pongo Pongu** - Bar and Snacks, DDP accepted, snacks are $3-$11 and drinks are $3.50-$13
**Satu'li Canteen** - Quick Service, DDP accepted, entrées are $12.50-$17

# MyMagic+

*MyMagic+ is Disney's tool for planning a seamless vacation. MyMagic+ is made up of three main components: My Disney Experience, FastPass+ (covered in the next chapter) and MagicBands.*

## My Disney Experience

This is a website and a mobile app that allow you to:
•Get you all the information you need in one place; plan as much, or as little, as you want.

•Make dining, FastPass+ and other reservations in advance
•See your in-park photos, including ride photos
•Purchase Memory Maker to receive access to all

photos and videos from your vacation
•Purchase park tickets
•See park maps
•See wait times for attractions and selected meet and greet experiences

## MagicBands

Disney resort hotel guests may purchase an RFID-enabled MagicBand that ties together all the features of MyMagic+. Up until 2021, these had been free but Disney has said the free ones will be phased out this year.

The MagicBand is worn on your wrist throughout your vacation. It allows you to check-in for Disney's Magical Express, open your Disney resort hotel room door, pay for food and merchandise, use Disney Dining Plans, make and use FastPass+ reservations, use Disney's PhotoPass service, have automatic on-ride photos with Memory Maker, and enter the theme parks and water parks.

MagicBands are shipped 10 to 30 days before arrival to US addresses, or to the resort if your reservation is made within 10 days of arrival. International visitors receive their MagicBand at hotel check-in.

If you are not staying at a Disney resort hotel, you can purchase a MagicBand for $14.99 from Walt Disney World Resort stores, although MagicBands do not do very much for non-Disney hotel guests except allow you to tap into the parks and attractions instead of using your park ticket, and linking photos and videos to PhotoPass and Memory Maker accounts.

**MagicBands & special events:**
Throughout the year, in-park events take place outside of regular park hours, and require a separate physical 'hard ticket' such as Magic Kingdom's Halloween and Christmas parties. You can seamlessly use your MagicBands during events.

You can link your separate 'hard ticket' admission ticket to your My Disney Experience account by entering the ticket number on the website or the app. If

you bought your ticket on the Disney website, you may find that it is already automatically linked. This allows you to enter the park with a MagicBand instead of using a paper ticket.

You will be given a physical 'event wristband' for special events at the park entrance if you enter after a certain time. Guests who enter the park before this time will need to present themselves at a designated location inside the park to pick up an event wristband. You must wear an event wristband during special events, as well as optionally wearing a MagicBand.

# FastPass+

*Walt Disney World offers a FREE time-saving system, called FastPass+.*

> ☼ **COVID-19 CHANGES:**
> **FastPass+ is suspended at all Walt Disney World theme parks. This information is presented for your reference for when the system returns (date unknown).**

## How to make FastPass+ reservations

The steps are similar on the My Disney Experience (MDE) website, the app, or the in-park FastPass+ kiosks.

Sign in to MDE. Link your park tickets and hotels. At in-park kiosks, just touch your MagicBand.

•Select 'FastPass+'. Choose the date and theme park you want to make a FP+ reservation for.
• Select the people you are making FP+ reservations for.
• Select a time for your FP+ reservations.
   o At Magic Kingdom, choose any three experiences.
   o At EPCOT, Animal Kingdom and Disney's Hollywood Studios, choose 1 attraction from Tier 1 and 2 attractions from Tier 2.

More information on these Tiers on page 68.
• You will see all available 1-hour FP+ reservation slots.
• You can make up to three advanced FP+ reservations per day for one theme park (but only one per ride).

When it is time to use your FP+ reservation, go to the attraction, tap your MagicBand or park ticket on the Mickey head by the FP+ entrance to enter the FP+ queue line which provides expedited attraction entry. The FP+ reservation is for a

specific booked time, except a 5-minute leeway before and 15 minutes after. If an attraction breaks down, the FP+ reservation is valid all day.

During your visit, you can add and change FP+ reservations at in-park kiosks or with the MDE app.

If you arrive without FP+ reservations, you can make up to 3 FP+ reservations at the park using one of the FP+ kiosks or the MDE app.

## When can I make FastPass+ reservations?

**Staying On-Site**
If you are staying at a Walt Disney World hotel, 60 days before your check-in date, you can make FastPass+ reservations for up to three experiences for each day of your vacation online via the MDE website or app.

If staying at a Disney hotel, you can make FastPass+ reservations for their whole stay (up to 14 days all at

once).

**Staying Off-Site**
If you are not staying at a Disney hotel, you can make FastPass+ reservations up to 30 days in advance. You must have bought your tickets before your visit begins and linked these on MDE (you will need to register for a free account).

Off-site guests need to visit

MDE daily 30 days before each day of their vacation.

**More Details**
You can make FastPass+ reservations starting at 7:00am Eastern Time either 30 or 60 days before your vacation. If you are not logged in at 7:00am EST, you will likely miss some of the most popular FastPass+ experiences.

> **Disney Club Level Extra FastPass+** - If you book Club Level at a Disney resort hotel, you can purchase an extra 3 FastPass+ reservations - for an additional $50 per person per day. These FastPass+ reservations can be made 90 days before your check-out date. This is not good value for money, in our opinion, but if you have very limited time, this may make sense. If that's not you, follow the tips in this chapter instead.

# "Additional" same-day FP+ reservations

• **Once you have used all 3 of your advanced FastPass+ reservations, you can make additional in-park FP+ reservations** on the MDE app or an in-park kiosk. Don't make your FP+ reservations for late in the day, so you can take advantage of these "additional" same-day FP+ reservations.

• **EPCOT, Animal Kingdom and Hollywood Studios use a tiered system** for your advanced reservations. After you have used all 3

initial FP+ reservations, you can "additional" same-day FP+ reservations for any attraction, regardless of its tier. The tier system does not apply to "additional reservations".

• **With the "additional" FP+ reservations**, you can choose any attraction at any park if it has a FP+ slot free – you do not have to be inside the park you want to use the FastPass+ in when making the reservation. For example, if you spend the morning at Magic

Kingdom Park using your pre-booked FastPass+ reservations and want to book a FastPass+ attraction at EPCOT, you can do this while at Magic Kingdom.

• **You can only make one "additional" reservation at a time**. Once your "additional" FastPass+ reservation has been used, you can make another FastPass+ reservation. Repeat this as many times as you want.

# Get a 'Hard-to-Get' FastPass+ Reservation?

Log into MDE's FastPass+ page at exactly 7:00am Eastern Time, either 30 days before your trip (for non-Disney hotel guests) or 60 days before (for Disney hotel guests). You must be logged in this early for the most popular FP+ experiences.

Even being logged in this far in advance, some FastPass+ reservations are very difficult to get – *Mickey & Minnie's Runaway Railway, Millennium Falcon: Smugglers Run, Frozen Ever After, Seven Dwarfs Mine Train, Slinky Dog* and *AVATAR: Flight of Passage* are some good examples.

If you cannot get a FastPass+ reservation by being early, there is a solution. This strategy works both with advance FastPass+ reservations and those made on the day.

**Gaming the System**
My Disney Experience

searches for FastPass+ availability for all members of your party at the same time.

So, if you want to visit Toy Story Mania and there are 4 people in your party, the system will look for a time slot for 4 people to ride together. If it cannot find a slot for 4 people, it will say there is no availability.

However, if you look for a slot for only 2 or 3 people, you may find availability.

You should look for a FP+ reservation for a lower number of people than are in your party first. Then, once you have confirmed that reservation, look for another reservation for the remaining party members.

With some luck, the reservation times will overlap and you can all ride together! If they do not overlap, take the FastPass+ reservations anyway and modify the times later - this is usually possible.

# List of FastPass+ Experiences

An asterisk (*) next to a ride name means it is a top pick for choosing as a FP+ reservation.

**Magic Kingdom:**
- Big Thunder Mtn Railroad
- Buzz Lightyear's Space Ranger Spin
- Dumbo the Flying Elephant
- Enchanted Tales with Belle
- Haunted Mansion
- "it's a small world"
- Jungle Cruise
- Mad Tea Party
- Meet Ariel at Ariel's Grotto
- Meet Cinderella
- Meet Rapunzel
- Meet Mickey Mouse
- Meet Tinker Bell
- Mickey's Philharmagic
- Monsters Inc. Laugh Floor
- Peter Pan's Flight*
- Pirates of the Caribbean
- Seven Dwarfs Mine Train*
- Space Mountain*
- Splash Mountain*
- The Barnstormer
- The Magic Carpets of Aladdin
- The Many Adventures of Winnie the Pooh
- Tomorrowland Speedway
- TRON Lightcyle Run (expected 2021)
- Under the Sea: Journey of the Little Mermaid

At Magic Kingdom, you can choose any combination of experiences. At EPCOT, Animal Kingdom and Hollywood Studios you choose one attraction from Tier 1, and two from Tier 2.

**Disney's Animal Kingdom:**
**Tier 1 (Choose one attraction):**
- Avatar Flight of Passage*
- Na'vi River Journey*

**Tier 2 (Choose two attractions):**
- Adventurers Outpost
- Dinosaur
- Expedition Everest*
- Festival of the Lion King
- Finding Nemo: The Musical
- It's Tough to be a Bug
- Kali River Rapids*
- Kilimanjaro Safaris
- Primeval Whirl
- Rivers of Light - We Go On
- Up! A Great Bird Adventure

**Disney's Hollywood Studios:**
**Tier 1 (Choose one attraction):**
- Mickey & Minnie's Runaway Railway*
- Millennium Falcon: Smugglers Run*
- Slinky Dog Dash*

**Tier 2 (Choose two attractions):**
- Alien Swirling Saucers
- Beauty and the Beast - Live on Stage
- Disney Junior Dance Party!
- Fantasmic!
- For the First Time in Forever: A Frozen Sing-Along Celebration
- Indiana Jones Epic Stunt Spectacular!
- Muppet*Vision 3D
- Rock 'n' Roller Coaster
- Star Tours
- The Twilight Zone Tower of Terror
- Toy Story Midway Mania!*
- Voyage of the Little Mermaid

**EPCOT:**
**Tier 1 (Choose one attraction):**
- Frozen Ever After*
- HarmonioUS
- Remy's Ratatouille Adventure (expected)*
- Soarin'*
- Test Track*

**Tier 2 (Choose two attractions):**
- Disney & Pixar Short Film Festival
- Journey into Imagination with Figment
- Living with the Land
- Mission: SPACE
- The Seas with Nemo & Friends
- Turtle Talk with Crush

# Park Touring Strategies

*This chapter is intended to help you tour the parks and reduce your time waiting in queue lines. It is not a complete touring plan but strategies of when to do certain attractions.*

## Before We Begin...

You should be at the park at least 30 minutes before the official opening time of each park, with your park ticket in hand, to make the most of these touring strategies.

**Top Tip 1**: The theme parks regularly allow guests in up to 45 minutes before the

published opening time, with select attractions open. Being at the park entrance early lets you take advantage of this 'secret early entry'.

**Top Tip 2**: As long as you are in a queue line by the closing time of a theme

park, you can experience the attraction, no matter how long the wait is. E.g. It is 9:59pm and the Magic Kingdom closes at 10:00pm and the wait time for *Buzz* is 25 minutes. Get in line now and you will still ride even though you will ride after the official park closing time.

## Magic Kingdom

**Big Thrills:**
**With FastPass+ suspended:**
Go to *Seven Dwarves Mine Train* first, followed by *Space Mountain, Big Thunder Mountain* and *Splash Mountain* in this order. These have the longest waits throughout the day - enjoy the rest of the park at your leisure.

When *Tron Lightcycle Run* opens, do this first then follow the above list.

**With FastPass+ available:**
Make reservations for P*eter Pan's Flight, Seven Dwarfs Mine Train* and *Jungle Cruise*. When *Tron Lightcycle Run* opens, swap Jungle Cruise out for this.

If you can't get an advanced FastPass+ reservation for *Seven Dwarfs Mine Train*, go there first and then follow the next step.

If you do have a *Seven Dwarfs Mine Train* reservation, the first thing you should do at park opening is to ride the three 'mountains' in this order: *Space Mountain, Big Thunder Mountain* and

*Splash Mountain*. You can often do all of these within the first hour of park opening. Later in the day, these often have waits of two hours each.

After 9:30pm (assuming *Happily Ever After* is showing at 10:00pm), most rides will have a line of 10 minutes or less – *Under the Sea, Buzz Lightyear* and *Winnie the Pooh* regularly have waits of about 60 minutes most of the day but have no wait in the evening.

The same also applies to *Peter Pan's Flight* which does not usually have a wait of more than 20 minutes this late at night (despite what may be posted as the wait time).

At shows such as *Carousel of Progress, Monsters Inc. Laugh Floor, Mickey's Philharmagic, Country Bear Jamboree* and *Enchanted Tiki Room*, you should never wait more than 15 minutes. If the wait time is longer, come back later.

**Kids' Favorites:**
**With FastPass+ suspended:**
Ride *Seven Dwarves Mine Train* first, followed by *Peter Pan*, then *Winnie the Pooh* and *Enchanted Tales with Belle in this order*. Work your way around the rest of the park.

**With FastPass+ available:**
Make reservations for *Seven Dwarfs Mine Train, Jungle Cruise* and *Enchanted Tales with Belle*. Those who want to meet the princesses in *Fairytale Hall* should make this their most important Fastpass+ reservation (substituting *Jungle Cruise*).

At park opening, ride *Peter Pan's Flight* first, followed by *The Barnstormer, Winnie the Pooh* and *Under the Sea*. You can usually do these four rides within the first 60 minutes of the park opening provided you keep up the pace. Work your way around Fantasyland.

The wait time for *"it's a small word"* rarely exceeds 25 minutes so you can do that at any point of the day; the same applies to all of the shows.

# EPCOT

**With FastPass+ suspended:**
Ride *Test Track* first, followed by *Soarin'*, followed by *Frozen Ever After*. When *Ratatouille* opens do this first, *Frozen* second, then *Test Track*, then *Soarin'*. Do the rest of the park at your own pace.

**With FastPass+ available:**
*Frozen Ever After* is EPCOT's second-newest ride and this ride usually has the longest wait in the park along with *Ratatouille*. You should make a FastPass+ reservation for either of these attractions in advance - you will leave the

other for the end of the day.

*Test Track* is the third most popular attraction in this park. Go here first as soon as the park opens.

Next, head over to *Soarin'*, and then ride *Mission: Space*. This will involve a lot of going back and forth but it is the best use of your time.

Once you have done these three rides, all the major long-lined rides are done - except *Frozen Ever After* and *Ratatouille*!

Alternatively, if you are happy splitting up your group, ride *Soarin'* first followed by *Test Track* in the Single Rider line.

The *Magic Eye Theater, The Seas with Nemo and Friends, Journey into Imagination with Figment* and *Living with the Land* very rarely have waits of over 20 minutes, with most of these being walk-ons all day long.

If the wait is longer than this for any of these attractions, then return later in the day.

# Disney's Hollywood Studios

**With FastPass+ suspended:**
Try and get a Boarding Group for *Star Wars: Rise of the Resistance* using the process described on pg 57.

Ride *Slinky Dog Dash* first, followed by *Toy Story Mania, Minnie's Runaway Railway, Rock 'n' Roller Coaster* and then *Tower of Terror*.

**With FastPass+ available:**
Try and get a Boarding Group for *Star Wars: Rise of*

the Resistance.
Assuming you have a FastPass+ reservation for *Slinky Dog* or *Mickey and Minnie's Runaway Railway*, at park opening, you should ride whichever one you don't have a Fastpass for. Then, ride *Toy Story Mania*.

Avoid this park on a day when it has morning Extra Magic Hours if you are not staying at a Disney hotel.

After *Midway Mania*, ride

*Rock 'n' Roller Coaster* and then *Tower of Terror*.

Most of the other attractions are shows – get there 20 minutes before.

*Voyage of the Little Mermaid* sometimes has waits of over 30 minutes. If so, come back later.

*Star Tours'* wait time fluctuates throughout the day, but you shouldn't wait for more than 20 minutes.

# Disney's Animal Kingdom

**With FastPass+ suspended:**
Ride *Flight of Passage*, then *Na'vi River Journey*, then *Expedition Everest* and *Kilimanjaro Safaris* next. Enjoy the rest of the park at your leisure.

**With FastPass+ available:**
Ideally, you should have a FastPass+ reservation for *AVATAR: Flight of Passage*. If so, head for *Na'vi River Journey*. If not, head straight to *AVATAR: Flight of Passage*

at park opening. Be at the park gates at least 1 hour before opening (not 30 minutes like the other parks). Then, follow this plan - save *Na'vi River Journey* for the very end of the day.

*Expedition Everest* should be next, followed by *Kilimanjaro Safaris* (the animals are most active in the morning!) and then *Kali River Rapids*.

On very hot days, waits for *Kali River Rapids* get long from 11:00am onwards. If this is a priority, make a FastPass+ reservation.

*DINOSAUR*'s wait time fluctuates during the day but you shouldn't wait more than 20 minutes. If it is longer, come back later.

Everything else is a show; turn up 15 to 20 minutes before the start time.

# Blizzard Beach Water Park
## Disney Water Park Basics and Tips

•Mats, inner tubes, life jackets, changing room, showers, car parking and floatation devices are free.
• Seating and cabanas can be reserved for a charge.
• Entry into one water park is $69.03 for adults and $62.84 for children, incl tax.
• Lockers are $10 for a small locker and $15 for a large locker. Towel rentals are $2.
• Children of diaper age must wear tight rubber pants over their diapers, or swimming diapers.

• Swimsuits with metal are not allowed on slides.
• Bring something to wear on your feet as the walkways become very hot!
• Arrive early to get a lounger with shade, or alternatively arrive in the afternoon when crowds will have thinned out.
• Buy a disposable waterproof camera for unforgettable pictures.
• If there is a thunderstorm, you will be asked to leave the water and all rides will

temporarily shut down. Brave it out, as thunderstorms are usually brief, and you will find a much emptier park when the attractions re-open.

 **COVID-19 CHANGES:**
Both Disney water parks are currently closed until at least March 2021.

## Reserved Seating and Cabanas

Two areas can be reserved – both require wristbands to access, given when checking in at the park:

•**Polar Patios** – There are 4 cabanas available to rent in this area accommodating up to 6 guests each. The cost varies between $225 and $340 plus tax, depending on the season. Additional guests can be added for $25

each. Cabanas include a one-day refillable drinks mug for each person, a cooler with ice and bottled water, lounge furniture, rental towels, private lockers and waiter service. Reservations can be made up to 180 days in advance by calling 407-WDW-PLAY. On the day reservations are subject to availability.

• **Lottawatta Lodge Picnic Umbrellas** – This area includes 2 lounge chairs, an umbrella, a small table and two towels. Pricing is between $40 and $60 plus tax for 2 to 4 people. Reservations can be made up to 180 days in advance by calling 407-WDW-PLAY. On the day reservations are subject to availability.

## Attractions
### Green Slope
**Summit Plummet** – Guests must be 48 inches (1.22m) or taller to ride. This is the park's premier attraction and at 120-feet tall is one of the tallest and fastest free-fall slides in the world. You will see it as you approach the park with riders braving speeds of up to 60 miles per hour!

**Teamboat Springs** – This ride is yet another record-breaker, being the longest "family white-water raft ride" in the world at 1,400 feet (427 m) in length. Guests board a big blue raft with handles and room for four to six people – and it is a wild, downhill ride from there! Infants may not ride.

**Slush Gusher** – Guests must be 48 inches (1.22m) or taller to ride. This body slide has you reaching speeds of up to 35 mph, as you follow its 250-foot long course. Due to its layout, it is one of only a few water slides where you really get some "air time".

# Red Slope

**Runoff Rapids** – These are a series of 600-foot inner tube slides – two are open-air and one is enclosed. There are multiple slides but you cannot race as all the slides are different lengths. Access to this attraction is via stairs only.

# Purple Slope

**Downhill Double Dipper** – Guests must be 48 inches (1.22m) or taller to ride. A racing slide where guests board inner tubes, push their tubes out and wait at the automated gates. When everyone is lined up, there is a countdown and the gates all open at once. At the bottom of the hill, each slide has its own timer to see who won the race. Great fun for competitive types.

**Snow Stormers** – This is a mat slide where guests lie on their stomachs on a toboggan style mat. There are 3 flumes and each is 350-feet long.

**Toboggan Racers** – This is the most competitive-looking of all the slides at Blizzard Beach. There are 8 identical lanes, each 250 feet long. Guests line up on their mats and stomachs and wait for the signal, then push off, race down the slopes and see who reaches the furthest, the fastest.

# Ground Level

**The Chairlift** – This is a one-way ride from Ground Level to the summit of Mount Gushmore where all the green slides are. Guests with disabilities may use the chairlift for return trips. Each wooden bench carries up to 3 people and the ride lasts about 4 minutes. There is an accessible Gondola too. Guests must be at least 32 inches tall to ride. To ride alone guests must be at least 48 inches (1.22m) tall.

**Cross Country Creek** – This is a lazy river that goes all the way around the park, totaling 3000 feet. There are seven entrances and exits and floating devices (inner tubes) are available at each of them. The journey takes 20 to 30 minutes for a full loop. Beware of the icy cave!

**Melt-Away Bay** – A one-acre wave pool with constant short bobbing waves.

**Tike's Peak** – This area features kiddie versions of some of the bigger slides. There is also a fountain play area themed to a snow castle and picnic benches.

Guests must be 48 inches (1.22m) tall or shorter.

**Ski Patrol Training Camp** – This area is split into several attractions: *Cool Runners* is an inner tube area, Leisure Pool has icebergs which kids under 12 can walk across, *Freezin' Pipe Springs* is a short body slide and *Fahrenheit Drops* is a T-bar drop attraction that drops guests that are under five feet (1.52 m) tall into 8.5 feet (2.6 m) deep water – being able to swim or using a floatation device is essential.

---

## DINING

**Avalunch** - Snacks and Quick Service, DDP accepted, entrées are $10-$11
**Cooling Hut** - Sandwiches, snacks, desserts and drinks, DDP accepted, prices are $4-$11
**Frostbite Freddy's Frozen Freshments** - Snacks, No DDP, entrées & desserts are $4.50-$12
**I.C. Expeditions** - Snacks, No DDP, snacks are $4.50-$14
**Lottawatta Lodge** - Snacks and Quick Service, DDP accepted, entrées are $8.50-$11
**Mini Donuts** - Snacks, donuts and drinks, No DDP, donuts are $5-$10
**Polar Pub** - Bar, serves alcoholic and non-alcoholic drinks, No DDP, $3-$11
**Warming Hut** - Snacks and Quick Service sandwiches, DDP accepted, entrées are $9-$11

# Typhoon Lagoon Water Park

*Typhoon Lagoon Water Park is home to North America's largest outdoor wave pool. The story goes that Typhoon Lagoon was once a tropical paradise when a typhoon came through and wreaked havoc, including "Miss Tilly", a boat that was flung onto the top of Mount Mayday during the typhoon. Every half an hour when the ship's bells sound, a geyser of water erupts into the air.*

## Typhoon Lagoon Basics

• Entry into Typhoon Lagoon is $69.03 for adults and $62.84 for children, including tax.
• Rental lockers are available throughout the park. The cost is $15 for a small locker and $20 for a large locker.
• Towels can be rented for $2.
• Lost children are taken to High 'N Dry Towels.

☼ **COVID-19 CHANGES:**
Both Disney water parks are currently closed until at least March 2021.

## Reserved Seating and Cabanas

Two areas can be reserved at Typhoon Lagoon – both require wristbands to access which are given when checking in at the park:
•**Beachcomer Shacks** – There are 4 cabanas available to rent here, accommodating up to 6 guests each. The cost varies between $240 and $345, including tax, depending on the season. Additional guests can be added for $25

each. Each cabana includes a one-day refillable drinks mug per person, a cooler with ice and bottled water, lounge furniture, rental towels, private lockers and waiter service. Reservations are made up to 180 days in advance at 407-WDW-PLAY. On the day reservations are subject to availability.

•**Getaway Glen** – This area includes 2 lounge chairs, an

umbrella, a small table and two towels and is priced between $43 and $49, including tax, for up to four people. Reservations can be made up to 180 days in advance by calling 407-WDW-PLAY. On the day reservations can be made at High N' Dry Towel Rental subject to availability. This is an option to guarantee a lounge chair, without turning up early.

## Surfing School at Typhoon Lagoon

Typhoon Lagoon's wave pool is the perfect place to learn to surf. Several surf schools are provided by carefully selected schools. These run on selected dates very early in the morning.

Classes are of up to 13 people with 2 instructors and are priced at $199 per person (including tax). Surfboards are provided.

Due to the early start time,

regular hotel transportation is not available, but resort hotel buses run by the time the class ends. Book up to 90 days in advance by calling 407-WDW-PLAY.

# Attractions

## Mount Mayday

**Humunga Kowabunga** – Guests must be 48 inches (1.22m) or taller to ride. Reach speeds of up to 39mph and slide down five stories on each of the three enclosed "speed slides".

**Gangplank Falls** – A family slide with inner tubes connected for 4 people.

**Storm Slides** – Three body slides that twist and turn leaving riders in a splash pool at the bottom.

**Mayday Falls** – A tube slide that creates the feeling of being in "rough rapids".

**Keelhaul Falls** – A tube slide that spirals through a waterfall and cave.

## Hideaway Bay

**Crush n' Gusher** – Guests must be 48 inches (1.22m) or taller to ride. A roller coaster-style water slide with one to three-person rafts available – here you go both downhill and uphill with the help of high-pressure jets.

This is great fun and there are three different slides to choose from. Next to this attraction, you will also find a beach area with lounge chairs and a small pool.

**Miss Fortune Falls** – Board this exciting family-raft attraction to spy the precious treasure artifacts collected by Captain Mary Oceaneer. This is the park's newest attraction - it opened in 2017.

## Typhoon Lagoon

Home of the huge signature wave pool and sandy beaches to relax on.

**Typhoon Lagoon Surf Pool** – This star park attraction is the North America's biggest outdoor wave pool. It alternates between 6-foot high surfing waves launched at 90 seconds intervals for 90 minutes, followed by small bobbing waves for 30 minutes.

Whatever setting the wave pool is on, waves are designed to be small by the time they reach the shore.

A chalkboard at the edge of the beach posts the day's wave schedule. Inner tubes are not permitted in the lagoon.

**Bay Slides** – Several slides for toddlers. Guests must be 60 inches or shorter to ride.

## Castaway Creek

A 2,100-foot lazy river that weaves through lush scenery around the whole park. Inner tubes are provided and a round trip takes 20 to 30 minutes.

## Ketchakiddee Creek

A play area for younger kids with waterspouts and a small sandy beach. Guests must be 48 inches or shorter to ride the small slides in this area.

---

### DINING

**Happy Landings Ice Cream** - Snacks, No DDP, desserts are $4.50-$14
**Leaning Palms** - Snacks and Quick Service, DDP accepted, entrées are $7.50-$13
**Let's Go Slurpin'** - Bar, No DDP, drinks are $6-$13
**Lowtide Lou's** - Snacks and Quick Service, DDP, accepted entrées are $10-$11
**Snack Shack** - Snacks, No DDP, snacks are $9.50-$11.50
**Typhoon Tilly's** - Snacks and Quick Service, Snacks, DDP accepted, entrées are $9.50-$11

# Disney Springs

*The Disney Springs area is an exciting metropolis of restaurants, theaters and shops.*

Disney Springs borders the south shore of Village Lake in the east-central portion of Walt Disney World. Self-parking at Disney Springs is free. Valet parking is $20. Disney runs buses to and from Disney Springs from all Disney resort hotels.

There are buses from the theme parks to Disney Springs from 4:00pm - but not from Disney Springs to the theme parks to avoid guests parking here for free and heading to the theme parks. To go from Disney Springs to a theme park you must go to a hotel first.

There is boat transportation around Disney Springs, but the whole area is very

walkable.

Bars and restaurants have varied opening and closing times but are usually open between 10:30am and 11:30pm (some locations open as early as 8:30am for breakfast).

Shops are generally open from 10:00am to 11:00pm Monday through Friday, and 10:00am to 11:30pm on weekends. Some locations are open later.

# Entertainment

**Amphicars** – At The Boathouse, you can enjoy a guided tour on an amphicar that drives both on land and water. Pricing is $125 for up to 3 people with your own personal captain. Available 10:00am to 10:00pm daily, weather permitting. $25 discount for shop or dining spends of over $50.

**Bibbidi Bobbidi Boutique** – A magical salon to transform your children into little princesses and princes. Prices range from $20 to $450, plus tax. For ages 3 and up. Currently closed due to COVID-19.

**Disney's Photopass Studio** – Add professional-style individual or family photo-shoots to your PhotoPass account at no extra cost.

**Marketplace Carousel** – A small carousel.

**Paradiso 37 Entertainment** – Live entertainment in the evenings.

**Raglan Road Live Music** – Live Irish-inspired music outside the venue.

## Cirque Du Soleil - Drawn to Life

Disney describes the new show, opening in 2021: "This new show follows the story of Julie, a courageous and determined girl who discovers an unexpected gift left by her late father: an unfinished animation piece. Guided by a surprising pencil, she embarks on an inspiring quest sprinkled with her Disney childhood memories. Through this journey, she learns to imagine new possibilities and animate the story of her future."

## AMC Movies

24 movie screens, with stadium-style seating in 18 theaters for unobstructed viewing. Includes six 'Fork & Screen' dine-in theaters.

## House of Blues

Live music every night including blues, jazz, country and rock. Also home to the famous Gospel Brunch on Sundays.

## Splitsville Luxury Lanes

A vintage, retro-style bowling alley with a fresh spin on music, dining and entertainment. Currently closed due to COVID-19.

## Aerophile - Balloon Flight

An iconic tethered balloon that sends guests soaring 400 feet into the sky, offering breathtaking views of the Walt Disney World Resort.

## NBA Experience

*NBA Experience* is the ultimate place for basketball fans. You can dribble, shoot and dunk as you practice your skills, play interactive trivia games about the sport, head inside the player locker rooms and on the Draft Day stage, and much more. Tickets are $34 plus tax each. Currently closed due to COVID-19.

# Dining - Drinks Lounges

• Dockside Margaritas – No DDP, drinks are $7.50-$17
• Jock Lindsey's Hangar Bar – No DDP, appetizers are $10-$12. Cocktails are up to $19.
• Rainforest Café Lava Lounge – appetizers are $11-$21, cocktails from $11.
• Stargazers Bar – No DDP, appetizers are $7-$11, drinks are $7-$110.

# Dining - Quick Service

• Blaze Fast-Fire'd Pizza – Delicious custom pizzas in 180 seconds, $8-$10 each.
• Cookes of Dublin – Irish food, entrées are $12-$15.
• D-Luxe Burger – American food, burgers are $10-$14.
• Earl of Sandwich – Sandwiches, salads and wraps are $6-$8.50.
• Food Truck Park – Disney Food Trucks selling food inspired by the parks. Each dish is $6 to $13.
• Morimoto Asia Street Food – Pan-Asian, entrées: $6-$14.
• Pepe by José Andrés – Spanish sandwiches, $8-$14.
• Pizza Ponte – Pizzas are $7-$8 for a slice or $9-$10 for a sandwich.
• The Polite Pig – American BBQ flavors, entrées: $12-$22.
• The Smokehouse at House of Blues – American food, entrées are $6-$14.
• Wolfgang Puck Express – entrées are $9-$20. Breakfast options: $8-$14.

# Dining - Specialty Food & Beverage and Snacks

• Amorette's Patisserie – No DDP, pastries, cakes and crepes are $7 to $75.
• AristoCrêpes – Crepes: $7-$9
• B.B. Wolf's Sausage Co. – Sausage snacks: $9.50-$14
• The Daily Poutine – Canadian food, poutine: $10.
• Disney's Candy Cauldron – Candy and chocolates.
• Erin McKenna's Bakery NYC – Snacks are $2-$10.50.
• The Ganachery – A chocolate lover's dream.
• Ghirardelli Soda Fountain – Desserts are $6-$13, drinks are $5-$9.
• Goofy's Candy Co. – Candy, cookies, chocolates, frozen drinks and more.
• Joffrey's Coffee & Tea Co. – Drinks are $3.50-$6. Alcoholic drinks are $12.
• Sprinkles – Cupcakes, No DDP, cupcakes: $5-$6, cookies: $3.50. There is even a Cupcake ATM.
• Starbucks – Drinks $3-$6.
• Vivoli il Gelato – Gelatos are $5.50-$7.50 and milkshakes are $10-$12.50. Serves Panini sandwiches, espresso drinks and gelato.
• Wetzel's Pretzels – Pretzels are $6-$10.
• YeSake – Snacks are $5.50-$10.

# Dining - Table Service

• AMC Disney Springs 24 Dine-In Theatres – No DDP, entrées are $11-$18.
• The Boathouse – American style, entrées are $13-$50. Upscale waterfront dining.
• Chef Art Smith's Homecomin' – Southern favorites from a glass-walled show kitchen and the Southern Shine Bar. Entrées are $18 to $30. At brunch, entrées are $17-$28.
• City Works Eatery & Pour House – Live sports bar. Brunch entrees are $15-$22. Lunch and dinner: $17-$29.
• The Edison – Themed to a 1920s-period power plant. American food, craft cocktails and live entertainment. Entrées are $18-$24 at lunch and $20-$38 at dinner. 21+ only after 10:00 p.m.
• Enzo's Hideaway – Italian. Entrées: $24-$43. Sunday evenings, a family-style feast is $45 per adult & $19 per child.
• Frontera Cocina –

American and Mexican food, entrées are $19-$38.
• House of Blues – American food, entrées are $16-$42.
• Jaleo by José Andrés – Spanish tapas cuisine. Entrees are $10 to $37.
• Maria & Enzo's – Italian cuisine, entrées are $17-$46 at brunch, $24-$46 at lunch and dinner.
• Morimoto Asia – Pan-Asian, Signature Dining, entrées are $19-$32. There is a lighter 'late night' menu with entrées at $13-$17.
• Paddlefish – Seafood, entrées are $17-$65.
• Paradiso 37 – Entrées are $17-$38.
• Planet Hollywood – American food, entrées are $16-$30.
• Rainforest Café – American food, entrées are $17-$37.
• Raglan Road Irish Pub and Restaurant – Irish food, entrées are $12-$24 at lunch, $14-$29 at dinner, $14-$22 at brunch.
• Splitsville Dining Room –

American food, entrées are $12-$26.
• STK Orlando – Rooftop Steakhouse, No DDP. Entrées are $11-$75 at lunch, $21-$253 at dinner, and $11-$74 at brunch.
• T-REX – American food, entrées are $18-$30.
• Terralina Crafted Italian – No DDP, entrées: $14-$44.
• Wolfgang Puck Bar & Grill – Mediterranean dishes. Entrees are $17-$24.
• Wine Bar George – No DDP, entrées are $13-$72, drinks are $9-$60.

# Shops

### Fashion and Sportswear
Stores include American Threads, Anthropologie, Columbia, DisneyStyle, Everything But Water, Fit2Run, francesca's, Free People, JOHNNY WAS, kate spade new york, LACOSTE, Levi's, Lilly Pulitzer, Lucky Brand, lululemon, NBA Store, Pelé Soccer, Shore, Stance, Superdry, Tommy Bahama, Tren-D, Under Armour, UNIQLO, Volcom and ZARA.

### Toys and Games
Stores include Dino-Store, The LEGO Store, Once Upon A Toy, and Star Wars Galactic Outpost, Star Wars Trading Post and Super Hero Headquarters.

### Jewelry and Accessories
Stores include ALEX AND ANI, Chapel Hats, Coach, Edward Beiner, Erwin Pearl, Kipling, Luxury of Time, Na Hoku, Oakley, PANDORA, Something Silver, Sunglass Icon, TUMI, UNOde50 and Vera Bradley.

### Footwear
Stores include Havaianas, Johnston & Murphy, Melissa Shoes, Sanuk, Sperry and UGG.

### Home, Decor, Gifts and Speciality
Stores include The Art Corner, The Art of Disney, The Boathouse BOATIQUE, Coca-Cola Store, Crystal Art, Disney's Days of Christmas,

Disney's Pin Traders, Disney's Wonderful World of Memories, House of Blues Gear Shop, Marketplace Co-Op, Mickey's Pantry, Orlando Harley-Davidson, Pop Gallery, Rainforest Café Retail Village, Ron Jon Surf Shop, Shop for Ireland, Sosa Family Cigars, The Store at Planet Hollywood, Sugarboo & Co. and World of Disney Store.

### Beauty and Health
Stores include The Art of Shaving, Basin, Kiehl's, M·A·C Cosmetics, L'Occitane en Provence, Origins, Savannah Bee Company and Sephora.

# Guests with Disabilities

⚙ **COVID-19 UPDATE:**
The Disability Access system is operating as normal as per the next page. There are no exemptions for mask-wearing including for any disabilities. If you need a break from wearing your mask, you may wish to enjoy one of Disney's Relaxation Station areas where you may sit socially distanced without wearing a mask. Check these on the park map.

## Mobility

The Walt Disney World Resort strives to allow all Guests to utilize the main attraction entrances whenever possible, allowing the ride queuing system to be as fair as possible for all guests whatever their physical or mental abilities.

However, accessibility does vary from attraction to attraction within the Disney Parks – disabled guests should ask a Cast Member at the entrance to an attraction for the appropriate entrance. Sometimes guests can remain in ECVs, other times they must transfer to a wheelchair, and other times they must transfer to a ride vehicle.

To rent a wheelchair, or ECV/motorized scooter for the day, proceed to the stroller shops located near the main entrance of each of the four theme parks, the Disney Springs Marketplace or the water parks. Guests may also bring their own into the parks.

If someone in your group with a disability needs to remain in a stroller while in the attraction queues, visit the Guest Relations lobby location near the entrance of any of the four theme parks to receive a "stroller as wheelchair" tag to be placed on the stroller.

Wheelchairs and ECVs rented at theme parks and the Disney Springs area are only for that specific location and must be returned before exiting. Length-of-stay rental tickets are available for a one-time payment, but wheelchairs or ECVs must still be returned before exiting each location.

Pricing is $12 per day for a wheelchair rental in the theme parks *(you can use one receipt for rentals across multiple theme parks on the same day)*. Multi-day rentals are also available at $10 per day. ECV rentals are $50 per day, plus a $20 refundable deposit in the theme parks. Outside vendors such as 'Buena Vista Scooters' rent ECVs at more affordable daily rates, usually from $30 to $40 per day.

All Walt Disney World resort transportation accommodates both wheelchairs and ECVs.

## Hearing

Guests with hearing disabilities have the following accommodations for them at the theme parks: Assistive Listening systems, Reflective Captioning, Sign Language interpretation, Text Typewriter telephones, Handheld Captioning, Video Captioning and written aids.

Not every system is available at every location so be sure to ask Cast Members for help explaining what is available to aid you.

Some attractions are equipped with reflective captioning – simply inform the attractions Cast Members when entering the theater or attraction, and they will activate this feature.

**WHAT ABOUT SPECIFIC INFORMATION?**
If you require specific information regarding the exact details of each attraction we strongly recommend you read Walt Disney World Resort's useful cognitive guide available at www.bit.ly/disndis.

# Visual

Guests with visual disabilities have the following accommodations for them at the theme parks: Audio Description devices, Braille guidebooks and digital audio tours.

# At the Resort Hotels

Examples of accommodations that are offered in resort hotels include wheelchair-accessible bathrooms, ramps and elevators, rooms designed for hearing impaired guests, and rooms that accommodate service animals. Accessible rooms can be booked online by using the "Accessible room" filter on the Walt Disney World Resort website, or by calling 407-939-7675 to discuss requirements in more detail.

# Disability Access Service (DAS)

The Disability Access Service (DAS) is designed for guests with disabilities (including non-apparent disabilities) that are not able to wait in a normal queue line – their privileges will also extend to their party.

DAS can be activated from Guest Relations at each theme park – no proof of disability is required, but the Cast Member will ask you several screening questions to determine eligibility.

At Guest Relations, the disabled guest will have their photo taken, asked how many guests are in their party (limited to 6 maximum). This information is linked to all MagicBands/tickets in the party. DAS will be activated for 14 consecutive days. After 14 consecutive days, a guest will need to revisit Guest Relations to re-activate the system.

**How does the system work?**
A disabled guest goes to an attraction (or another party member on behalf of the DAS guest) and asks the Cast Member there to use DAS – the ride attendant will issue the guest with a return time (this will be the current wait time, minus 10 minutes). E.g. it is 2:00pm and the wait time for an attraction is 45 minutes – the guest will be issued with a 2:35pm return time. The return time is generated automatically by the system and cannot be changed by the Cast Member.

Until the return time, this guest can do whatever they wish. They can ride the attraction at any time after the return time. So, a guest could use their 2:35pm return time slot at 3:00pm, or they could return to ride at exactly 2:35pm. There is no early entry grace period for DAS reservations.

Guests can view their return time on the My Disney Experience app or using in-park FastPass+ kiosks. This return time cannot be edited by guests or Cast Members.

Only one return time may be active at once – as soon as it has been used, another return time can be made for another attraction.

Alternatively, guests can cancel a return time, and reserve another attraction. The system can be combined with FastPass+ and guests will still get the full FP+ entitlements, in addition to being able to use the system.

When it is time to ride, the DAS-eligible guest must be present at the ride entrance along with their party. They scan their MagicBand or park ticket and the whole of the party will be allowed entry. The reader will turn blue and the Cast Member will confirm that the DAS-eligible guest is present and will be riding. If the DAS-eligible guest does not wish to ride, the rest of the party must use the normal standby entrance.

There is a separate program for children with life-threatening illnesses, and wish-granting organizations. Disney says any guest who feels this system will not work for them should visit Guest Relations to work out a solution.

# Activities Outside the Parks

*Walt Disney World offers much more than just theme parks and water parks. This chapter delves into this world of other possibilities.*

## ESPN Wide World of Sports

This 200-acre sports complex hosts both professional and amateur sports games. Facilities include three baseball fields, six NBA-sized basketball courts, softball courts, tennis courts, a track and field center, and beach volleyball courts.

Access to most amateur events can be purchased at the Box Office on-site. Adult tickets are priced at $19.50 and children's tickets are priced at $14.50. Park tickets with the 'Park Hopper Plus' option may be used for entry to some events.

Access to the venue is available via limited buses from Disney's All-Star Resorts, Disney's Caribbean Beach Resort and Disney's Pop Century Resort. Free parking is also available.

Information on tickets is available on 407-939-GAME or at www.disneyworldsports.com

## Miniature Golf

The mini-golf courses at the Walt Disney World Resort are surprisingly well priced - $14 for adults and $12 per child per round.

### Disney's Fantasia Miniature Golf
This mini-golf location consists of two different courses – Fantasia Gardens and Fantasia Fairways, both themed to the animated classic Fantasia.

Fantasia Gardens is perfect for those who are new to mini golf and kids; expect water effects, creative obstacles and great theming.

Fantasia Fairways is for the more experienced mini-golfers and can be more frustrating for younger children.

Fantasia Mini-golf is open daily from 10:00am to 11:00pm.

These courses are located on EPCOT Resort Boulevard behind the Walt Disney World Swan Hotel and can be reached by taking a bus to either the Boardwalk Inn or Swan hotels and walking from there – ask for directions at the concierge desks at either resort.

### Disney's Winter Summerland Miniature Golf
This mini-golf location features two different courses – a winter-themed course and a summer-themed course.

At the winter course your job is to make your way through the course towards the 'North Hole', while at the summer course you are surrounded by beach theming.

The two courses are right next door to Blizzard Beach Water Park. You can drive there or take one of the resort buses. From Blizzard Beach, it is less than a 5-minute walk to Winter Summerland mini-golf.

# Golf

The Walt Disney World Resort is home to four world-class golf courses that have won several awards – three of these are 18-holes and there is also a more leisurely 9-hole course.

The courses are:
- **Magnolia Golf Course** – The main hazard on this 18-hole course is water. Golf Digest rated this course 4 stars.
- **Lake Buena Vista Golf Course** – This 18-hole golf course has hosted the PGA Tour, the LPGA Tour and USGA events. Golf Digest rated this course 4 stars.
- **Palm Golf Course** – An 18-hole golf course.
- **Oak Trail Golf Course** – This 9-hole family-friendly golf course is a walking distance course with a par of 36. There are even junior tees for the smaller family members. Pull carts can be rented.

**Pricing:**
- Pricing varies from $35 to $75 per person for each of the three 18-hole courses. The price for the Oak Trail Golf Course is $19 per junior (under 18) and $35 for adults. Disney hotel guests pay the lowest prices.
- Sunrise and Sunset rates are also often available at $35 for the 9-hole courses.
- 2-round and 3-round discounted passes are also available for purchase.
- Free transportation to all courses is available for Disney hotel guests.
- Professional club rentals are available for a fee: $40-$65 for Magnolia, Buena Vista and Palm, and $15 for Oak Trail (a partial set). Junior club rentals are free of charge at Oak Trail.
- 45-minute-long personal golf lessons are available. The pricing is $75 for adults and $50 for juniors aged 17 and under.
- Replay rates are available with a 50% discount off the full rate. Replays must be on the same day and cannot be reserved in advance.

**Other information:**
- The use of a golf cart is included in your greens fee for the courses. Carts are designed to be shared by two guests. To provide an enjoyable pace of play, players must use golf carts on the 3 championship courses.
- Proper golf attire is required at all the golf courses; denim jeans or casual shorts are not permitted.
- Reservations at Disney's Magnolia Golf Course are recommended but not necessary. Walk-up golfers will try to be accommodated.
- Disney recommends you arrive at least 30 minutes before your tee time to allow for check-in, cart assignment and a warm-up.
- For more detailed information on golfing, and to book tee times contact Disney directly on 407-WDW-GOLF or visit www.golfwdw.com.

# Free activities outside the parks

**1. Visit the resort hotels**
If you love the theming in the parks, visit the hotels. From the relaxing beach at the Polynesian Village Resort to the forest of the Wilderness Lodge, there is something for everyone. Combine your trip to a resort with a meal. You do not need to be staying at the resorts to visit them. It is possible to spend three or four days simply visiting and exploring the dozens of Disney hotels. A must-do!

**2. Movies under the stars**
The Disney resort hotels offer nightly screenings of a Disney movie under the stars on a big screen. Chill out on one of the sun loungers sipping a cocktail while watching Toy Story or Fantasia.

**3. Visit Disney's Boardwalk**
This is a fun seaside-themed resort boardwalk area. You can often enjoy live entertainment such as jugglers, or you can explore the Boardwalk Resort and grab a bite to eat in one of the many restaurants.

**4. Enjoy the Transportation**
The monorail, ferryboat and The Skyliner all provide great views of the resort. The hidden gems, however, are the boats between certain resorts and theme parks, such as the boat from the Wilderness Lodge to Fort Wilderness. This is a great, quaint, relaxing trip where all you see around you are trees and the lake. Boats from Port Orleans, Old Key West and Saratoga Springs to Disney Springs

also offer relaxing moments.

**5. Sing around a camp-fire**
*(suspended during COVID)*
Every evening, you can join Chip n' Dale in a sing-along around a camp-fire at Fort Wilderness Resort. There are optional marshmallows to buy to roast on the fire. After the camp-fire, there is a movie under the stars.

**6. Watch a free parade**
*(suspended during COVID)*
Every evening, the nighttime Electrical Water Pageant sails on the Seven Seas Lagoon. It is a simple flotilla, but it is worth seeing. AllEars.net provides the following info on the timing:
• Polynesian Village Resort: 9:00pm
• Grand Floridian: 9:15pm
• Wilderness Lodge: 9:35pm
• Fort Wilderness: 9:45pm
• Contemporary Resort: 10:05pm
• Magic Kingdom Park: 10:20pm (during extended park hours).
When Magic Kingdom's fireworks are at 9:00pm, the Electrical Water Pageant runs 7 to 20 minutes later.

**7. Fireworks from Polynesian Village Resort**
*(suspended during COVID)*
Nothing can match standing in front of Cinderella Castle and seeing the nightly fireworks explode up close but for a different view, go to beach at the Polynesian Village Resort.

You can't see the projections from this distance but they do play the show music out of speakers at the Polynesian Village Resort

walkway by the beach when the show begins. Arrive 45 minutes before the show.

**8. Do a free Walt Disney World Resort hotel tour**
Disney runs free tours of certain resort hotels. You do not need to be staying at the resorts to take these tours nor need reservations. The 20-minute Sanaa Cultural Tour explores the Sanaa restaurant. It runs at 4:00pm daily. This tour may end with a tasty treat too! Call (407) 938-3000 to confirm this tour's schedule.

The Wonders of the Wilderness Lodge Tour is a 1-hour tour on the backstory and design of the Wilderness Lodge Resort. The tour runs Wednesdays to Saturdays at 9:00am. Call (407) 824-3200 to confirm this tour's schedule.

The Culinary Tour at Animal Kingdom Lodge is a food tour of the Boma and Jiko restaurants of about 30 minutes. You get to sample some of the food. Call (407) 938-3000 to confirm this tour's schedule.

# Meeting the Characters

⚙ **COVID-19 CHANGES:**
Character meets are all currently suspended - you may see characters at a distance in the parks but not up-close. Character Dining is suspended except for modified experiences at Garden Grill Restaurant, Hollywood & Vine, Topolino's Terrace and Chef Mickey's.

In total, about 60 different characters meet in the parks daily. Some characters are 'random' appearances that are not published on the park schedule, others are 'scheduled' meets where you queue and take a photo, others are elaborate indoor experiences, and others like *Enchanted Tales with Belle* are more like interactive shows. You can also meet characters at select dining experiences. If you need help finding a character, ask a Cast Member. Or, simply call 407-WDW-INFO.

Here we list character appearances that happen regularly and usually daily - these may change.

## Magic Kingdom Park

•**Aladdin and Princess Jasmine** – Near Aladdin's Magic Carpets in Adventureland.
• **Alice in Wonderland** – By Mad Tea Party in Fantasyland
• **Ariel** – In Ariel's Grotto in Fantasyland.
• **Belle** – For those who take part in the show, you can take a photo at Enchanted Tales with Belle.
• **Buzz Lightyear** – Next to Buzz Lightyear's Space Ranger Spin.
• **Cinderella** – In Princess Fairytale Hall in Fantasyland.
• **Daisy and Donald Duck** – At Pete's Silly Sideshow in Fantasyland.
• **Elena of Avalor** – In Princess Fairytale Hall.
• **Gaston** – Outside Gaston's Tavern in Fantasyland.
• **Goofy** – At Pete's Silly

Sideshow in Fantasyland.
• **Mary Poppins** – In Liberty Square Gazebo.
• **Merida** – In Fairytale Garden
• **Mickey Mouse** – Town Square Theater.
• **Minnie Mouse** – At Pete's Silly Sideshow.
• **Pluto** – At Pete's Silly Sideshow.
• **Peter Pan and Wendy** – Near Peter Pan's Flight.
• **Rapunzel** – All day in Princess Fairytale Hall.
• **Stitch** - In Tomorrowland
• **Tiana** – At Princess Fairytale Hall.
• **Tinker Bell** (and fairy friends) – At Town Square Theater.
• **Winnie the Pooh and Tigger** – Near The Many Adventures of Winnie the Pooh.

## EPCOT

• **Aladdin and Princess Jasmine** – Morocco Pavilion
• **Anna and Elsa** – Norway Pavilion
• **Alice (in Wonderland)** – UK Pavilion
• **Aurora** - France Pavilion
• **Belle** – France Pavilion
• **Daisy Duck** – Near Spaceship Earth
• **Donald Duck** – Mexico

Pavilion
• **Goofy** – Near the park entrance.
• **Joy** (From 'Inside Out') – in the Imagination pavilion.
• **Mary Poppins** – UK Pavilion
• **Mickey Mouse** – In the waiting area of Disney-Pixar Short Film Festival
• **Minnie Mouse** – World

Showcase Gazebo
• **Mulan** – China Pavilion
• **Pluto** – Near the park entrance.
• **Snow White** – Germany Pavilion
• **Winnie the Pooh** – UK Pavilion
• **Wreck-it Ralph and Venellope** – In the Imagination pavilion.

### Character Tips
•Character waits can be as long as for rides.
•Do not force children to interact with characters.
• Chat to the face characters and get an insight into their lives.
•There are more characters out in the mornings and early afternoons than in the evenings.
•Characters have limited vision. They may not be able to see what is even directly in front of them.
•Characters can sign anything; except what you are wearing.
•Characters may not hold children or infants.
•Do not be angry if the character needs to leave for a few minutes.
•Fur characters can't talk.
•Be courteous and do not hurt the characters.

# Disney's Hollywood Studios

- **Buzz Lightyear, Woody & Green Army Men** – Near Toy Story Mania
- **Cars Characters** – In Cars Courtyard
- **Chip & Dale** – Near Crossroads of the World.
- **Doc McStuffins and Fancy**

**Nancy** – Outside Disney Jr.
- **Edna Mode** – At An Incredible Celebration.
- **Mickey** (in his Sorcerer costume) **and Minnie** – At Red Carpet Dreams.
- **Olaf** – At Celebrity Spotlight, by Echo Lake.

- **Pluto** – In Animation Courtyard.
- **Star Wars Characters** – At Star Wars Launch Bay.
- **Sulley** – At Walt Disney Presents.
- **The Incredibles** – In Pixar Place.

# Disney's Animal Kingdom

- **Chip and Dale** – In Dinoland USA.
- **Donald and Daisy**– In Dinoland USA.
- **Dug and Russell** (from Up) – Near the entrance to It's Tough to be a Bug.
- **Goofy** – In Dinoland USA.
- **Mickey and Minnie** – At

Adventurers Outpost.
- **Pocahontas** – At Discovery Island Trails
- **Pluto** – In Dinoland USA.
- **Rafiki and Timon** – At Rafiki's Planet Watch.
- **Scrooge McDuck** – In Dinoland USA.

# Character Dining

- **Alice in Wonderland** – 1900 Park Fare, Grand Floridian (Breakfast only);
- **Beast** – Be Our Guest Restaurant (dinner only, Magic Kingdom)
- **Chip n Dale** – Garden Grill (EPCOT)
- **Cinderella** (and maybe Prince Charming) – 1900 Park Fare, Grand Floridian (Dinner only); Cinderella's Royal Table (Magic Kingdom); Akershus Royal Banquet Hall (Norway pavilion, EPCOT)
- **Donald Duck** – Tusker House in Disney's Animal Kingdom (and other ducks – Breakfast and Lunch); Cape May Café at Beach Club (Breakfast only); Chef Mickey's at Contemporary Resort (Brunch and Dinner)
- **Disney Junior Characters** (Sofia the First and Doc McStuffins) – Hollywood and Vine (Breakfast and Lunch, Disney's Hollywood

Studios)
- **Lady Tremaine, Anastasia and Drizella** – 1900 Park Fare, Grand Floridian (Dinner)
- **Lilo and Stitch** – Ohana's Best Friends Breakfast, Polynesian Village Resort.
- **Goofy** – Cape May Café at Beach Club (Breakfast only); Chef Mickey's at Contemporary Resort (Brunch and Dinner); Tusker House at Animal Kingdom
- **Mad Hatter** – 1900 Park Fare, Grand Floridian (Breakfast only);
- **Mary Poppins** – 1900 Park Fare, Grand Floridian (Breakfast only), Princess Storybook Meals (Norway pavilion, EPCOT)
- **Mickey Mouse** – Garden Grill (EPCOT); Chef Mickey's at Contemporary Resort (Brunch and Dinner); Ohana's Best Friends Breakfast, Polynesian Village Resort;

- **Minnie Mouse** – Cape May Café, Beach Club (Breakfast only); Chef Mickey's at Contemporary Resort (Brunch and Dinner)
- **Pluto** – Garden Grill (EPCOT); Chef Mickey's at Contemporary Resort (Brunch and Dinner); Ohana's Best Friends Breakfast, Polynesian Village Resort.
- **The Princesses** – Cinderella's Royal Table (Magic Kingdom); Akershus Royal Banquet Hall (Norway Pavilion, EPCOT)
- **Winnie the Pooh, Tigger, Piglet and Eeyore** – Crystal Palace (Magic Kingdom), 1900 Park Fare, Grand Floridian (Breakfast only). None of these character appearances are guaranteed but they are a good indication of who you can expect to see and where.

# Doing Disney on a Budget

*Visiting Walt Disney World is not exactly cheap, but it can be done on a budget, and you can still have a fantastic trip while saving some cash.*

## Planning

**1. Staying On-Site** – Do you need a Disney hotel? They are convenient but are often more expensive than off-site hotels. Remember to factor in costs like resort fees, taxes, parking and transportation when comparing.

**2. Buy an annual pass** – If you plan on visiting more than once in the same year, buying an annual pass can be a great money saver. If staying off-site, you will not need to pay for parking at the parks with an annual pass. It can also save you a lot of money on hotels, dining and merchandise.

**3. Wait for a special offer** – Walt Disney World often runs special offers – whether it is discounted room prices or free dining, so keep an eye out for these. Free dining offers, in particular, can save you a lot of money.

**4. Downgrade your hotel** – Do you need a luxury Disney hotel? Will you use the amenities you are paying for? If not, then downgrade to somewhere less expensive.

**5. Tickets** – Buy tickets online at reputable websites, e.g., undercovertourist.com – there are savings of up to $77 per person compared to buying from Disney. European visitors should consider the Ultimate Tickets, instead of buying tickets at American prices.

**6. Quieter times** – By visiting when the parks are less busy, you can do more each day and spend fewer days in the parks. See our quiet times section of this guide. Tickets are also cheaper during off-peak periods.

**7. Don't bring a car** – Disney hotel parking costs $15-$33 per night. Theme park parking is $25-$50 per day (theme park parking is free for Disney hotel guests).

## At the Parks

**1. Do not purchase a Dining Plan** – Although the Dining Plans claim savings of up to 40%, if you don't eat a lot, or eat cheaper dishes, it's cheaper to pay for each meal individually.

**2. Packed lunches** – You can make your own meals, such as sandwiches, and take them into the parks. If you have a car, drive to a nearby supermarket for supplies.

**3. Eat meals off-site** – Drive off-property and eat outside of Walt Disney World. Food is usually a fraction of the cost of the parks.

**4. Table Service at lunch** – Table Service, character and buffet meals are often cheaper at lunch than at dinner. The food on offer may be different or the same.

**5. Take your own photos** – Don't pay $15 or $20 for a character photo. Take one yourself, ask another guest, or ask a Cast Member (not permitted during COVID-19) who will be happy to help.

**6. Take your own merch** – If your child is likely to want to buy a dress or outfit in the parks, these are substantially cheaper online, at supermarkets or anywhere outside Walt Disney World. Buy them and pack them secretly. Give your child the costume once you arrive. The same applies to Disney plushes and toys.

**7. More affordable meals** – Some meals are better value than others. Kids' Quick Service meals, for example, offer great value and include a drink, whereas adult meals do not. Everything can be ordered a la carte - remove the fries if you don't want them. Or, have a late lunch buffet and then a smaller snack for dinner.

# Dining

*There is a huge variety of places to eat at Walt Disney World, from sandwiches to fast food to Table Service dining, character buffets to signature options.*

## Restaurant Types

**Buffet restaurants** – Fill up your plate from the food offered as many times as you want. A variation is "family style" meals where servers come around to tables and offer food.

**Quick Service** – Fast food. Everything from burgers and fries, to chicken to pizza and pasta, as well as more exotic options.

**Table Service** – Restaurants where you order from a menu, and are served by a waiter/server.

**Character buffets** – All-you-can-eat locations where characters visit each table to interact while you dine.

**Signature Dining Experiences** – The most exquisite dining experiences. These require two Table Service credits for guests on Disney Dining Plans.

**Dinner Shows** – A meal (usually buffet or family-style) is included in the price, as well as your entertainment for the evening. Dinner shows cost two Table Service credits for guests on Dining Plans.

## Disney Dining Plans

*These are currently not available during COVID-19.* Disney Dining Plans are pre-paid dining credits. Dining Plans are available to guests who book a vacation package with park tickets and a hotel, and Disney Vacation Club bookings.

You are allotted a number of 'credits' for each night of your stay for Table Service meals, Quick Service meals and Snacks. The number of credits depends on the plan. Redeemed credits for meals.

You are given all your credits as a lump sum at the start of your trip; you choose how you use these by 11:59pm on check out day.

Disney claims you can save up to 40% by purchasing the Dining Plans but this relies on you always eating the most expensive menu items. You must book the Disney Dining Plans for the whole of your stay. You can get around this with two back-to-back hotel reservations, and only adding a Dining Plan to one.

Gratuities are not included with the dining plans except for Dinner Shows, Private In-Room Dining, and Cinderella's Royal Table.

Merchandise or photo products that are offered at some Character Dining meals are not included.

Reservations are strongly recommended for all Table Service restaurants - check menus at Disney.go.com/dining in advance to decide.

**Top Tip:** Present your MagicBand before ordering – restaurants often have a menu specifically for guests on Disney Dining Plans.

**Mobile Ordering:** Many of the Quick Service restaurants allow you to order and pay using My Disney Experience without waiting in line. You will be notified when your food is ready. This saves you time during peak hours. During COVID, many Quick Service locations exclusively use Mobile Ordering.

Here we list what is included per night of your stay with each Dining Plan for 2020. (Prices are per night and include tax - these offerings may change slightly for 2021 when they relaunch)

**Quick-Service Dining Plan**
$55 per adult, $26 per child (ages 3-9).
• 2 Quick Service meals (entrée and non-alcoholic beverage)
• 2 Snacks
• 1 refillable resort mug per stay (worth $20)

**Dining Plan**
$78.01 per adult, $30.51 per child.
• 1 Quick Service meal
• 1 Table Service meal (entrée and non-alcoholic beverage at breakfast OR entrée, dessert and non-alcoholic beverage at lunch and dinner. At buffets, you get access to the full buffet and a drink)
• 2 Snacks
• 1 refillable resort mug per stay (worth

**Dining Plan Plus**
$94.60 per adult, $35 per child.
• 2 Table Service or Quick Service meals. (For Table Service: entrée and non-alcoholic beverage at breakfast OR entrée, dessert and non-alcoholic beverage at lunch and dinner. At buffets, you get access to the full buffet and a drink)
• 2 Snacks
• 1 refillable resort mug per stay (worth $20)

**Deluxe Dining Plan**
$119 per adult, $47.50 per child.
• 3 Table Service or Quick Service meals. You can choose for maximum flexibility. You also get an appetizer at Table Service locations, in addition to an entrée, dessert and non-alcoholic beverage.
• 2 Snacks
• 1 refillable resort mug per stay (worth $20)

At the end of your meal, when you ask for the check, you will receive a receipt stating how many credits you used for that meal and how many remain. If you have bought several Dining Plans together, this number is the sum of all your party's credits. You are free to order off-menu items and pay for these separately.

# Reservations and Cancellations

At Table Service restaurants, we strongly recommend reservations. These can be made up to 180 days (60 days during COVID-19) in advance at 407-WDW-DINE or online. At popular dining locations, such as Cinderella's Royal Table, you need to make reservations exactly 180 days (60 days during COVID-19) in advance to dine at peak times.

A credit/debit card is required for dining reservations. Cancellations should be made the day before by 11:59pm; a $10 per person charge applies to no-shows.

Guests can also make last-minute dining reservations up to 20 minutes in advance using My Disney Experience.

# Dress Codes

The following have a business casual dress code:
• Artist Point at Disney's Wilderness Lodge
• California Grill at the Contemporary Resort
• Cítricos at the Grand Floridian Resort & Spa
• Flying Fish Cafe at Disney's BoardWalk
• Jiko – The Cooking Place at Animal Kingdom Lodge
• Monsieur Paul at EPCOT
• Narcoossee's at Disney's Grand Floridian Resort & Spa
• Takumi-Tei at EPCOT
• Yachtsman Steakhouse at Yacht and Beach Club Resorts

**Men's Dress Code:** Dress slacks, jeans, pants, or dress shorts, short- or long-sleeved shirt with a collar or a t-shirt is required. Jackets are optional.

**Ladies Dress Code**: Jeans, skirt, or dress shorts with a blouse, sweater or t-shirt, or a dress required.

**Not permitted:** Tank tops, swimsuits or cover-ups, hats for men, cut-offs, torn clothing, or t-shirts with offensive words or graphics. Victoria and Albert's has a much stricter dress code - enquire when reserving.

# Park Services

*Many things can make or break a Walt Disney World vacation. This chapter covers important things to consider such as when to visit, and park services.*

## PhotoPass and Memory Maker

In the theme parks, you will find photographers ready to take your photo at major landmarks, at character meets and other locations.

**PhotoPass:**
PhotoPass works with a special card which you are given, at no cost, the first time you have a photo taken. You then use this same card every time you take photos, handing it to the photographer to scan. Once your trip is over, enter the code on your PhotoPass card into the PhotoPass website to see all your photos. From there, you can add your photos to souvenirs, order individual prints or pay for photo downloads.

**Memory Maker:**
Memory Maker is a photo package that allows you to purchase all your PhotoPass photos at once. This includes in-park photos, character photos, dining photos and on-ride photos.

Photos are available from the day they were taken until 45 days later. You have 30 days from the date of your first download to take more pictures with your

Memory Maker account.

It is available in advance for $169 or at Walt Disney World for $199. If you have a MagicBand, tap it each time to get your photos in the park. You can also buy a physical CD archive with all your pictures for an extra $30, or download the photos for free.

Guests who wear a MagicBand on rides have their attraction photos automatically added to their My Disney Experience account without needing to stop at the ride photo counter. The ride photo at *Frozen Ever After* is exclusive to MagicBand wearers.

Also, riders with MagicBands on *The Twilight Zone: Tower of Terror* and *Seven Dwarfs Mine Train* have an on-ride video added to their account.

Although on-ride photos are usually linked automatically, it is still worth adding them manually as there can be errors. To do this, when you see the photo screens, tap your MagicBand on the reader below your photo.

A one-day Memory Maker package is available for $69. Guests can purchase the 'Memory Maker One Day' via the My Disney Experience app after having linked one photo.

**Top Tip 1**: Pre-purchase Memory Maker in advance at disneyworld.Disney.go.com/memory-maker/ to save $30. This must be done at least 3 days before your first photo is taken.

**Top Tip 2**: Take a photo of your PhotoPass card and its barcode, so if you lose the card you still have access to all the photos on it.

**Top Tip 3**: You can have multiple PhotoPass cards and add them all to one online account in one go.

## On-ride Photos

Many rides have specially placed cameras positioned to take perfectly framed photos of you on the ride. After the ride, you can

purchase these photos and save the memory.

You do not have to buy on-ride photos straight after

your ride; you can pick them up at any time during the day - remember your number at the ride exit. If you like the photo - buy it!

# Single Rider Queue Lines

*Single Rider Lines are not available during COVID-19.*
One of the best ways to significantly reduce your time waiting in queue lines is to use the Single Rider line instead of the regular standby queue line. This is a completely separate queue line that is used to fill free spaces on ride vehicles - guests who join this line will ride individually.

As an example of how the system works: if a ride vehicle can seat 8 people and a group of 4 turns up, followed by a group of 3 in the regular standby line, then a guest from the Single Rider line fills the space.

If the park gets extremely busy then Single Rider lines can be closed when the wait for Single Riders is the same or greater than the regular line, undermining its purpose. If the park is not very busy then sometimes these queue lines do not operate either.
Groups can use the Single Rider queue line; they will not ride with each other but can still meet after riding at the exit of the ride.

The following rides have single rider queue lines:
• Expedition Everest (Animal Kingdom)
• Rock n Roller Coaster (Hollywood Studios)
• Test Track (EPCOT)
• Remy's Ratatouille Adventure (EPCOT)
• Millennium Falcon: Smugglers Run (Hollywood Studios)

# Extra Magic Hours

*Extra Magic Hours are not available during COVID-19.*

Each day, Disney resort hotel guests are allowed 1-hour early entry into one theme park or can stay up to 2 hours after regular park closing at another park.

During these extended opening hours, wait times for rides are typically much shorter than during the day. Each member of your party needs a valid resort ID to access attractions during these extended hours.

The exact parks open during Extra Magic Hours (EMH) vary week to week and can be seen online up to 6 months in advance on the Walt Disney World website.

**How can I get Extra Magic Hours?**
They are available exclusively to guests staying at Walt Disney World resort hotels and select partner properties.

**What rides are available during EMH?**
Unfortunately, not all rides are open during these extended hours, but most popular rides (not shows)

are open - Disney does not publish an exact list.

*Star Wars: Rise of the Resistance* is not available during Extra Magic Hours.

# Rider Switch

Rider Switch is a system that enables a group to take turns riding an attraction while only needing to wait once. An example use is when a child is too small and adults take turns riding so the other can stay with the child.

To use Rider Switch, ask a Cast Member at an attraction entrance to use it.

Group 1 (for example, the father) will go through the normal queue line and Group 2 (for example, the mother) will be given a return time as a digital Rider Switch Pass on their park tickets or MagicBands. The return time will start roughly when Group 1 has returned and this return time lasts for 1h10m.

Once Group 1 has ridden, Group 2 passes the child to Group 1 and enters the ride through the FastPass+ entrance. Up to 3 people may ride with this pass. Rider Switch is available at all attractions with a minimum height limit.

# When to Visit

Crowds vary significantly from season to season and even day to day. The difference in a single day can save you hundreds of dollars and hours of waiting. You need to consider public holidays and school vacations in the U.S.A. and surrounding countries, the weather, pricing and more to find the best time to go.

**Major Holidays in 2021 :**
• 1st to 3rd January: New Year's Day & School Break
• 18th to 21st January: Martin Luther King Jr. Day and Weekend

• 12th to 24th February: Presidents Day & School Break
• 12th March to 8th April: Spring Break and Easter
• 28th to 31st May: Memorial Day Weekend
• Mid-June to Mid-August: Summer School Break (particularly busy around 4th July)
• 3rd to 7th September: Labor Day Weekend
• 8th to 12th October: Columbus Day Weekend
• 5th to 15th November: Veterans Day Week
• 19th to 29th November: Thanksgiving Week

• 17th December to 3rd January: Christmas and New Year's

**Best times to visit in 2021:**
• Early to mid-January
• Between Presidents Day and Spring Break
• Mid-April to mid-May (avoiding Easter and Spring Break)
• Late-May to Mid-June
• Mid-August to early-October (avoiding Labor Day Weekend, humid in August)
• End of November to mid-December

# Park Regulations

Here are some notable park regulations which you should be aware of:
• Proper attire, including shoes and shirts, must be worn. Anyone wearing inappropriate attire may be removed from the park.
• Smoking (including vaping) is not allowed in the parks.
• Guests under age 14 must be accompanied by another guest aged 14 or older to enter the theme parks and water parks.

• Recreational devices with wheels such as skateboards, scooters, skates or shoes with built-in wheels are not permitted.
• Strollers larger than 31" x 52" are not permitted.
• Any item of baggage or a cooler larger than 24" x 15" 18" is not permitted in the parks.
• Trailer-like items pushed or towed by a person or a machine are not permitted.
• Weapons, masks (except

face covering during COVID-19), folding chairs, large tripods, glass containers, alcoholic beverages, illegal substances, and animals that are not service animals are not permitted.
• Balloons, plastic straws and drink lids are not permitted at Disney's Animal Kingdom Park for the safety of the animals.
• Selfie sticks are banned from all Disney theme parks and water parks.

# Stroller Rentals

Strollers can be rented at the entrance to the four theme parks.

A single stroller, for children of 50lbs or less, is $15 per day, or $13 as part of a multi-day purchase.

A double stroller for children of 100lbs or less is $31 per day, or $27 as part of a multi-day purchase.

Strollers must be returned on the same day and cannot leave the theme parks.

You can use the same receipt to hire strollers at all four theme parks on the same day and only pay once. Strollers can also be rented at Disney Springs.

# 'Play Disney Parks' App

At some point you will find yourself in a queue line wondering how to pass the time - Disney has the answer with the free 'Play Disney Parks' app. This includes ride-specific games and trivia, music, and other cool interactive features. Plus, the app can let you interact with things outside the queue lines - such as many of the elements in Star Wars: Galaxy's Edge.

# Useful Phone Numbers

- **Main Street USA Barber Shop Appointments:** 407-824-6550
- **Central Lost and Found:** 407-824-4245
- **Central Reservations Office (CRO):** 407-934-7639
- **Disney Dining Reservations:** 407-WDW-DINE
- **Main Disney Switchboard:** 407-824-2222
- **Firework Cruises:** 407-939-7529

- **Golf:** 407-WDW-GOLF
- **Guest Services Mail Order:** 407-363-6200
- **Kennel:** 407-824-6568
- **Resort Medical Care:** 407-648-9234
- **Recreation:** 407-WDW-PLAY
- **Reservations:** 407-934-7639
- **Tours:** 407-WDW-TOUR
- **Walt Disney World Florist and Gift Basket Department:** 407-827-3505

(disneyflorist.com)
- **Walt Disney World Transportation:** 407-824-4321
- **WDW Operation Information** (Hours etc.): 407-WDW-INFO

To dial the USA from international locations, you will need to add '+1' before these phone numbers.

# Height Restrictions

Although we cover height restrictions throughout the parks section of this travel guide, this section gives you an overview of all the height restrictions in one place.

Do not try to fraudulently increase the apparent height of your child through heels or other measures.

Attractions Cast Members will ask for these to be removed before measuring.

Height restrictions are in place for the safety of all guests. No exceptions are made.

- Alien Swirling Saucers – Disney's Hollywood Studios – 32" (0.81m)
- Tomorrowland Speedway – Magic Kingdom Park – 32" (0.81m) to ride with an adult, or 54" (1.37m) to drive alone.
- Kali River Rapids – Animal Kingdom Park – 38" (0.97m)
- Slinky Dog Dash – Disney's Hollywood Studios – 38" (0.97m)
- Seven Dwarfs Mine Train – Magic Kingdom Park – 38" (0.97m)

- Millennium Falcon: Smugglers Run – Disney's Hollywood Studios – 38" (0.97m)
- Star Wars: Rise of the Resistance  – Disney's Hollywood Studios – 40" (1.02m)
- Big Thunder Mountain Railroad – Magic Kingdom Park – 40" (1.02m)
- Splash Mountain – Magic Kingdom Park – 40" (1.02m)
- Dinosaur – Animal Kingdom Park – 40" (1.02m)
- Star Tours – Disney's Hollywood Studios – 40" (1.02m)
- The Twilight Zone: Tower of Terror – Disney's Hollywood Studios – 40" (1.02m)
- Soarin' – EPCOT – 40" (1.02m)

- Expedition Everest – Animal Kingdom Park – 44" (1.12m)
- Mission: SPACE – EPCOT – 44" (1.12m)
- Space Mountain – Magic Kingdom Park – 44" (1.12m)
- Avatar Flight of Passage – Animal Kingdom Park – 44 inches (1.12m)
- Primeval Whirl – Animal Kingdom Park – 48" (1.22m)
- Rock 'n' Roller Coaster – Disney's Hollywood Studios – 48" (1.22m)
- TRON Lightcycle Run – EPCOT – 48" (1.22m) [expected height limit]

Additional height and weight restrictions apply at the Disney water parks.

# Spend Less Time Waiting

**1. Disney hotel guests** - At Disney hotels (and select other hotels), you get Extra Magic Hours (EMH) which give you one hours' early entry into one theme park each day, or you can stay up to two hours in another park in the evening. Most popular attractions are open.

Morning Extra Magic Hours are extremely valuable, as most people do not want to get up early, so you can hit many of the headline attractions in this first hour! Evening Extra Magic Hours are busier than the morning ones but ride waits are less than during regular hours.

**2. Visit a non-EMH park** – Disney's 30,000+ on-site hotel rooms mean the park with evening Extra Magic Hours is much busier than others. Go to a different park in the day, and visit the park with EMH only during the extended opening hours – you need a park hopper ticket. If you don't have EMHs, avoid parks on their EMHs day as they are busy with no extra benefit to you.

**3. Use Character Breakfast entrances at park opening** – Look for the park entrances marked "Character Breakfast". These are for guests eating in-park character breakfasts until park opening. From park opening, they are open to everyone!

**4. See our 'When to Visit' section** – If you are going on New Year's Day, expect to wait a lot longer than in the middle of September.

**5. The Parks Open Early** – Magic Kingdom Park opens 1 hour before the scheduled opening time. You wait in front of Cinderella Castle until the opening show. You can explore Main Street, U.S.A. during this time.

EPCOT frequently opens its gates 15 minutes or more before its official opening time. Some rides will be running straight away. Disney's Hollywood Studios opens its gates 15 to 45 minutes before the official opening time. Some rides run straight away.

At Disney's Animal Kingdom Park, gates usually open 30 to 45 minutes before the official time. *Kilimanjaro Safaris, Expedition Everest* and *Avatar Flight of Passage* usually open soon after this.

**6. Do the popular rides first** – If you arrive at park opening, ride popular attractions in the first hour! Head to these first.
- Magic Kingdom Park: *TRON Lightcyle Run, Seven Dwarfs Mine Train, Peter Pan's Flight* and *Space Mountain.*
- EPCOT: *Frozen Ever After, Ratatouille,* and *Test Track.*
- Disney's Hollywood Studios: *Slinky Dog Dash, Mickey and Minnie's Runaway Railway* and *Toy Story Midway Mania.*
- Disney's Animal Kingdom Park: A*vatar Flight of Passage, Na'vi River Journey* and *Expedition Everest.*

**7. Post-firework riding** – Check when the nighttime show is performed. If the park remains open after,

you can ride attractions until the park closes. At night, WAITS should be minimal. If you want a last-minute ride, get in the queue line before park closing to ride!

**8. Ride outdoor rides during the rain** – Outside rides such as *Dumbo, Slinky Dog Dash, Splash Mountain* and *Big Thunder Mountain* have much shorter waits when it is raining. During lightning, outdoor attractions temporarily stop operation.

**9. Go shopping at the start or end of the day** – Even when the park is officially closed in the evening, shops on Main Street, U.S.A., and other major shops in other parks stay open until most guests have left. Or, do your shopping at Disney Springs! Better yet, visit your resort hotel's own Disney store.

**10. Extra paid options** - Disney offers early entry to certain attractions for an extra fee ($89 per adult/$79 per child) with its Early Morning Magic event on select dates. Breakfast is also included [suspended during COVID-19].

# Guided Tours

*Get a different perspective of Walt Disney World with one of the many guided tours on offer. Go behind the scenes at the theme parks, scuba dive or enjoy a private safari.*

☼ **COVID-19 UPDATE:**
As of Dec 2020, only Wilderness Back Trail and VIP Tours operate. All other tours are suspended.

## Resort-Wide

**Backstage Magic – $275 per person (7 hours)**
Discover the heritage, secrets and daily operations of Walt Disney World. At EPCOT, explore the inner workings of *The American Adventure*. At Magic Kingdom, discover hidden details on Main Street, U.S.A., and the legendary underground "Utilidoor" tunnels. At Disney's Hollywood Studios learn how Imagineers thrill on *The Twilight Zone: Tower of Terror*, and visit Creative Costuming. Visit Central Shops and meet skilled craftspeople; Disney's Wilderness Lodge for a complimentary lunch, and then see the botanical side of the resort. Ages 16+.

**Disney's Yuletide Fantasy – Magic Kingdom – $148 (3 hours 30 minutes)**
On this festive tour, you will meet the "elves" who create the decorations for the parks and hotels; explore World Showcase and hear how holidays are celebrated around the globe; get an up-close look at the trimmings of Main Street, U.S.A; and visit a hotel to learn how the holiday atmosphere is created. Offered only on select dates in November and December. Ages 16+.

**Escape to Walt's Wilderness – $109 per person (5 hours)**
Begin with a boat tour from the Contemporary Resort as your guide shares stories of Walt Disney's passion for nature. Along the way, wildlife guides and binoculars help spot the wildlife. At Fort Wilderness, a bonfire and camp-style breakfast await. A wagon ride is next, followed by an archery lesson, and then a hike in the woods. Recommended for ages 7+.

**Disney's Holiday D-Lights – $259 per person (5 hours)**
At EPCOT witness the Candlelight Processional, and at Magic Kingdom take in the charm of the holiday trimmings on Main Street, U.S.A. and behold Cinderella Castle, transformed into an ice palace for the holidays. Meet the team responsible for turning the entire Resort into a winter wonderland. A light holiday-themed buffet is also included with your tour. Ages 16+.

**The Ultimate Day of Thrills (6 to 7 hours) and The Ultimate Day for Young Families (6 to 7 hours) – $299 per person**
These are two separate tours that include experiencing a certain number of attractions such as *Seven Dwarfs Mine Train, Toy Story Midway Mania!* and *Expedition Everest*. The Ultimate Day for Young Families – A VIP Tour Experience offers attractions that are specifically accessible to young children. Both tours include a meal at a Table Service restaurant.

## At the Resort Hotels

**Animal Kingdom Lodge Starlight Safari – $70 per person (1 hour)**
Climb aboard a sturdy, open-sided safari vehicle with night vision goggles to make the most of your animal-viewing extravaganza. From gazelles and giraffes to ostriches and zebras, prepare yourself for a few all-new memories as you discover different kinds of animal activity at each stop. You will even get a chance to see the inner-workings of the hotels, including their animal-friendly Cast Members!

**Sense of Africa – $250 per person (3.5 hours)**
A typical tour begins with a unique twist on breakfast at Boma -Flavors of Africa, followed by encounters with animals such as okapi, giraffe, ostriches and red river hogs.

**Savor the Savannah: Evening Safari Experience – $169 per person (2 hours)**
Your safari begins with a journey deep into the heart of the Harambe Wildlife Reserve to one of the most secluded and breathtaking private viewing areas of the Savannah. While savoring the Savannah scenery, indulge in a sampling of African-inspired tapas, paired with regional drinks.

**Disney Family Culinary Adventure – $175 per adult, $125 child (ages 9-12)**
Head backstage at the Contemporary Resort for an interactive evening with Disney chefs, hands-on cooking and a festive, five-course dinner. The evening starts with an introduction to the catering kitchen. Guests put on aprons, hats and gloves and are divided into cooking groups and move from station to station. Then, it's time to eat as each course is served.

**Wilderness Back Trail Adventure – $96 per person (2 hours)**
Navigate a variety of surfaces from paved paths to woodland trails as you complete a 2-hour circuit with stops at Disney's Wilderness Lodge, the Tri-Circle-D Ranch stables, and Bay Lake. Your guide shares trivia and anecdotes. Riders must weigh 100 to 250lbs. Ages 16+.

# Magic Kingdom

**Walt Disney: Marceline to Magic Kingdom Tour – $35 per person (3 hrs)**
On this walking tour, discover the secrets behind the magic. Your guide will share little-known facts about Walt, as well as the design and operation of classic attractions. This insider's look at the history of Magic Kingdom Park is perfect for the avid Disney fan and offers a lighter alternative to the more in-depth Keys to the Kingdom tour. Ages 12+. Guests under 18 must be accompanied by a paying adult.

**Keys to the Kingdom Tour – Magic Kingdom – $99 per person (5 hours)**
Uncover the hidden secrets of classic attractions, access the underground "Utilidoor" tunnels, discover little-known facts, trivia and other exciting tidbits about the park, explore the parade floats storage area, and enjoy your choice of lunch entrée at Columbia Harbour House. Photography is strictly prohibited. Ages 16+.

**Disney's Family Magic Tour – Magic Kingdom – $34 per person (2 hours)**
Aguided scavenger hunt collecting clues as an unforgettable adventure magically unfolds around you. Follow your guide as you make your way through Magic Kingdom, picking up clue after clue while unlocking a memorable quest. This adventure is best suited for Guests 4 to 10 years of age. Guests 16 years of age and under must be accompanied by a paying adult.

**Disney's The Magic Behind Our Steam Trains Tour – Magic Kingdom – $54 per person (3 hours)**
On this 3-hour tour sure to delight railroad enthusiasts, you ride the rails around the park in a fully restored antique freight train, gain exclusive backstage access to the roundhouse, where the steam engines are stored and serviced, discover what it takes to keep these trains in top working order and hear about Walt Disney's lifelong passion for steam trains.

# Disney's Animal Kingdom

**Wild Africa Trek – Disney's Animal Kingdom – $189 per person (3 hrs)**
Explore the Safi River Valley. See hippos and crocodiles ten feet below as you cross a shaky rope bridge, secured to an overhead track with a harness. Ride in a rugged safari vehicle over an open savannah teeming with native African creatures. A trained photographer takes digital photos throughout the adventure – a complimentary service. After working up an appetite, indulge in some African-inspired snacks.

**Backstage Tales – Disney's Animal Kingdom – $90 per person (3 hours 45 minutes)**
Explore backstage animal-housing areas, and the Animal Nutrition Center and see how over 4 tons of food are prepared and distributed each day, tour the state-of-the-art veterinary hospital, and learn how Disney promotes wildlife conservation and animal well-being. Ages 12+.

# EPCOT

### Behind the Seeds – EPCOT - $16 child / $20 adult (1 hour)
This tour of the fish farm and four greenhouses in The Land Pavilion is perfect for anyone with an interest in gardening or natural sciences. Visit a fish farm during feeding time and see American alligators, release ladybugs into a greenhouse, see gigantic fruits and vegetables and unusual crops from around the world and discover the latest plant-growing techniques.

### Disney's Dolphins in Depth – EPCOT – $206 per person (3 hours)
Talk to the expert trainers and researchers who work with EPCOT's bottlenose dolphins daily. Gain a greater appreciation of these creatures as you interact with dolphins in waist-deep water, see how Disney cares for the dolphins day to day, view backstage areas and learn how the dolphins are trained. You will not swim with dolphins. Ages 13+.

### EPCOT DiveQuest – $186 per person (3 hours)
Take the plunge at the 5.7-million-gallon saltwater aquarium, and swim with over 6,000 sea creatures. Clear waters and the absence of currents give you amazing views of dolphins, rays and sharks. With the pavilion's giant windows, family and friends can watch. About 40 minutes of the tour is on the dive. You also tour the backstage infrastructure that filters and maintains this vast manmade ocean. All guests must be SCUBA-certified. Ages 10+.

**Tour reservations and cancellations:**
Reservations are strongly recommended for all tours and for most of them is a requirement. These can be made up to 90 days in advance. Call 407-WDW-TOUR to book. You will forfeit the entire price of your tour if you no-show or cancel within 2 days of your reservation. For VIP Tours, if you cancel within this time, the cancellation fee will be 2 hours at the booked rate. The phone number to call to book VIP Tours is 407-560-4033.

**Additional tour notes:**
The itinerary, content, duration and availability of tours are subject to change without notice. If your tour travels backstage, no cameras, video equipment, or cell phones may be used during that portion of the tour. Photography is allowed and encouraged in non-backstage areas.

# VIP Tour Services

With your VIP Tour Guide, enjoy maximum fun with minimal fuss – the Disney vacation of a lifetime.

The team at Disney's VIP Tour Services plan the most efficient, enjoyable way for your group (up to 10 people) to see and do what's on your list. Just tell Disney what you want, and they will create an itinerary!

Your VIP Tour Guide meets you at your Disney hotel room door in a private vehicle and whisks you to the park of your choice. You enjoy a flexible start time; visits to multiple theme parks in a day, if desired; the ability to experience attractions efficiently, even repeatedly; VIP seating for parades, select stage shows and nighttime spectaculars; shared insight from your VIP Tour Guide, and a completely customized experience based on your preferences.

**VIP Tour Pricing:**
The pricing of a VIP tour varies between $425 and $625 per hour, depending on the season. Book at least 72 hours in advance and up to 90 days maximum. Tours have a minimum duration of 6 hours and your party may include up to 10 people. Parties larger than 10 require multiple guides.

# Seasonal Events

*There is always something unique to do at Walt Disney World. Due to COVID-19 vent details are very limited for 2021 and may change from the schedules below.*

## Walt Disney World Marathon - Jan 7 to Jan 10, 2021

This annual event features a 26.2-mile adventure race through all four Disney theme parks – Magic Kingdom Park, EPCOT, Disney's Hollywood Studios and Disney's Animal Kingdom. There is also a half marathon. Also included in the weekend is 'Goofy's Race and a Half Challenge,' which combines Saturday's half marathon and Sunday's full marathon for 39.3 miles of fun.

There is also a 5km run, the Walt Disney World 10K, and the Dopey Challenge, where participants run the 5K, 10K, half marathon and marathon (48.6 miles over four days). In 2021, this is a virtual event.

## EPCOT International Festival of the Arts - Jan 8 to Feb 22, 2021

At the EPCOT International Festival of the Arts you can explore the visual arts with galleries, workshops and seminars. Then try new food with the culinary arts. Finally, enjoy performing arts from acrobatics to living statues.

A collaboration with Disney Theatrical brings an exciting new showcase of favorite music and Broadway talent to the America Gardens Theatre stage bi-weekly.

## Princess Half Marathon Weekend - Feb 18-21, 2021

This predominantly women's Half Marathon brings guests of all ages together to celebrate all the qualities a princess possesses.
The weekend features a two-day health and fitness expo geared towards women, a family fun run of 5km and kids' races.

Guests can also run a 10K, and the Glass Slipper Challenge, where you run the 10K and half marathon over two days. In 2021, this is a virtual event.

## Star Wars Rival Run Weekend - Apr 15-18, 2021

Runners who join the Galactic Empire will enjoy a true Star Wars experience, including Dark side-inspired medals and merchandise throughout the weekend.

This event includes a 5K, 10K, kids races, and half marathon, plus a special challenge for completing the 10K and half marathon called the Star Wars Rival Run Challenge!

## EPCOT International Flower & Garden Festival - March to June 2021

Future World and World Showcase bloom with more than 30 million colorful blossoms, interactive garden activities for kids and workshops with gardening experts during this annual spring festival at EPCOT.

While exploring the themed gardens, guests can taste sweets and savories from food-and-beverage marketplaces around World Showcase Lagoon. Plus, musical entertainment pairs perfectly with brilliant botanicals during a complimentary concert. Disney gardeners lead weekend how-to Gardening Seminars at the Festival Center, where guests also can pick up signature festival merchandise.

When the sun sets, illuminated topiary and play

gardens glow brightly for an after-dark festival experience.

# Mickey's Not-So-Scary Halloween Party - 2021 dates TBC

A family-friendly fright-fest in Magic Kingdom Park featuring a parade, trick-or-treating, face painting, and more.

You can expect: a Villains show on the Castle Forecourt stage; a dead barbershop quartet in Frontierland; and Mickey's "Boo-to-You" Halloween Parade with the Headless Horseman. The night wouldn't be complete without 'Disney's Not So Spooky Spectacular', a ghoulish firework where Jack Skellington lights up the sky.

Mickey's Not-So-Scary Halloween Party also

features treat trails where more candy is given out per guest than we could eat in an entire year.

Mickey's Not-So-Scary Halloween Parties are typically held from 7:00pm to midnight on select dates from late August to October 31st.

This party is a separately ticketed event from standard park admission. Ticket prices in 2020 (before the event was canceled) started at $85 per adult and $80 per child, and rose to $149 and $144 respectively, excluding tax.

Peak date nights are more

expensive than non-peak nights. Tickets often sell out in advance and reservations are highly recommended.

If COVID-19 restrictions have eased, 2021's Halloween event will be broadly similar. In 2020, this event was canceled.

# EPCOT International Food & Wine Festival - 2021 dates TBC

Savor fine wines and delectable cuisine during the EPCOT International Food & Wine Festival featuring live entertainment such as the 'Eat to the Beat' concert series, guest chefs, culinary demonstrations, seminars and more.

Festival highlights include 35 international food and beverage marketplaces; signature dining experiences with world-renowned chefs; exciting culinary demonstrations and beverage seminars; the Eat to the Beat concert

series; more than 270 chefs including Disney chefs and culinary stars; and the Party for the Senses grand tasting events on Saturday evenings.

With so much to see and do, you can come back to the festival again and again and discover something new each time!

Most of the festival entertainment is included in regular park admission. Food and drink are an extra charge. There are over 250 food-and-beverage items —

each tapas-sized portion or drink is priced at $4 to $10.

2021 dates are unconfirmed but expect to see this event from mid-summer to mid-November.

# Disney Wine & Dine Half Marathon - 2021 dates TBC

The ultimate "Runners' Night Out" features a half marathon. After finishing, runners and their guests can celebrate their accomplishments at an exclusive after hours' party. The weekend also includes kids' races, a 5K family fun run, and a health and fitness expo.

2021 dates are not yet confirmed but expect this to take place on the last weekend of October or the first weekend of November.

# Mickey's Very Merry Christmas Party - Nov & Dec 2021

This party allows guests to delight in some holiday cheer on select evenings throughout November and December. This is an extra ticketed event.

As well as being able to experience the attractions throughout the park and meet characters, there are extra exclusive party-only experiences.

During the party, guests can experience: the castle sparkling with thousands of white lights; Mickey's Once Upon A Christmastime Parade featuring classic Disney characters, elves, toy soldiers and even Santa himself; Holiday Wishes, a breath-taking music and fireworks show; A Totally Tomorrowland Christmas;

the Mickey's Most Merriest Celebration Show; A Frozen Holiday Wish castle lighting; snowfall on Main Street, U.S.A. and much more! Guests also get complimentary hot cocoa and cookies all night long.

Mickey's Very Merry Christmas Parties are typically held from 7:00pm to select dates from early November to late December.

This party is a separately ticketed event from standard park admission. Ticket prices in 2020 (before the event was canceled) started at $105 per adult and $100 per child, and rose to $148 and $143 respectively, including tax.

After the last party takes place, all the entertainment from the party (except the complimentary snacks) is available to all guests in regular theme park admission. However, if you do wait until late December, expect the parks to be very busy and hotel room prices at their peak.

If COVID-19 restrictions have eased, 2021's event will be broadly similar. In 2020, this event was canceled.

# EPCOT: International Festival of the Holidays - Late November to Late December

There is a lot of entertainment for the Holiday season at EPCOT it is all included with EPCOT park admission.

The Candlelight Processional is a retelling of the Christmas story by a celebrity narrator who is accompanied by a 50-piece orchestra and a choir. The 2018 event runs nightly at The America Gardens Theater. It is presented three times per night at 5:00pm, 6:45pm and 8:15pm.

The Processional was canceled in 2020. In 2019 the line-up of narrators includes Neil Patrick Harris, Whoopi Goldberg and Geena Davis.

Each year, *JOYFUL! A Gospel Celebration of the Season* blends the soulful expressiveness of Gospel and inspirational music with the sounds of jazz, R&B and urban music at the Future World Fountain Stage.

The World Showcase comes alive with the nighttime spectacular *IllumiNations: Reflections of Earth* with a unique finale celebrating the season.

Other festive Holiday offerings include a Gingerbread Village at The Land pavilion, with sweet recreations of Walt Disney World Resort's theme park icons, plenty of holiday merchandise and food and beverage offerings around

World Showcase.

Guests can also celebrate each country's holiday traditions with storytellers at each pavilion during Holidays Around the World including Father Christmas at the UK Pavilion, Mr. & Mrs. Claus, Hanukkah traditions and Kwanzaa celebrations at the American Adventure and much more.

# The Holidays: Magic Kingdom, Resorts, Animal Kingdom, Hollywood Studios & Disney Springs - Nov & Dec

Walt Disney World is aglitter during the Holiday season with dazzling lights, spirited songs and snow flurries.

Here's what is in store: the Mickey's Very Merry Christmas Party at Magic Kingdom (an extra ticketed event); Candlelight Processional at EPCOT (included in theme park admission); plus, caroling, tree lighting ceremonies, decorations, and visits by Santa, included in your theme park admission.

Most details over these next pages have not yet been confirmed to be returning in 2021, but event details are broadly similar year on year.

**Magic Kingdom Park:**
At Magic Kingdom, guests can expect a Holiday version of the *Jungle Cruise* entitled *Jingle Cruise* with a revised script and new décors on the attraction.

What's more, Santa's elves transform the Magic Kingdom into a winter wonderland with festive wreaths, bows, garlands, sparkling lights, parades and towering Christmas trees. The fun includes the *Holiday Wishes* nighttime fireworks spectacular, plus characters dressed up for the holidays.

Also at Magic Kingdom, during a live show, Cinderella Castle is transformed in a glistening ice palace for the holidays — thanks to a special effects spectacle bathing the castle in 200,000 shimmering white lights.

Additionally, from late December, *Mickey's Once Upon a Christmastime Parade* is presented to day guests in the park in place of *Festival of Fantasy*.

**The Resorts:**
At Fort Wilderness Resort, you can enjoy a holiday sleigh ride through the woodland nightly from late November to late December. Sleighs hold up to 4 adults (or two adults and 3 children). The 25-minute ride is $84.

Disney's Grand Floridian has a 16-foot-high Victorian gingerbread house located in the lobby.

Disney's Beach Club hosts an incredible gingerbread carousel display, accompanied by the smell of Christmas treats.

Disney's Contemporary and Disney's Boardwalk Inn have their own gingerbread displays.

Wilderness Lodge and Animal Kingdom Lodge showcase breath-taking Christmas trees towering inside the resorts.

**Disney's Animal Kingdom:**
At Disney's Animal Kingdom, meet *Mickey and Minnie at Adventurers Outpost* for a special photo opportunity with the duo dress in their holiday best.

**Disney Springs:**
At Disney Springs, you can see enhanced holiday entertainment, specialty foods and festive décor.

Santa will be there too, of course.

**Disney's Hollywood Studios:**
"Jingle Bell, Jingle BAM!" is a festive nighttime show featuring fireworks, special effects, snow, music and projections of Disney's most cherished characters on the Chinese Theater.

Sunset Seasons Greetings is another nighttime projection show featuring lots of snow.

Guests can also meet Santa Claus from early November to Christmas Eve. From December 25th to December 31st, you can meet Santa Goofy instead.

**New Year's Eve:**
EPCOT and Magic Kingdom get very busy for New Year's Eve and you can expect the parks to fill to capacity by midday, at which point no further guests are allowed in. There is no extra cost for access on this date, but certain private events are at hotels and other locations. The parks are best avoided at this time of year as they are very crowded and wait times are astronomical. The 2021 event will be broadly similar.

# A Special Thanks

*Thank you very much for reading our travel guide to Walt Disney World. We hope that we have made a big difference to your vacation and you have found some tips that will save you time and money! Remember to take this guide with you while you are on vacation and use it in the parks.*

If you have any questions or feedback us, please use the 'Contact Us' section on our website at www.independentguidebooks.com. Please also check out our Youtube channel - type in "Independent Guides - Disney and Theme Park Videos"

If you have enjoyed this guide, you will want to check out:
• The Independent Guide to Universal Orlando
• The Independent Guide to Universal Studios Hollywood
• The Independent Guide to Disneyland
• The Independent Guide to Disneyland Paris
• The Independent Guide to Tokyo Disney Resort
• The Independent Guide to Shanghai Disneyland
• The Independent Guide to Hong Kong Disneyland
• The Independent Guide to London
• The Independent Guide to New York City
• The Independent Guide to Tokyo
• The Independent Guide to Hong Kong

Have a magical day!

## Photo Credits:
The following photos have been used under a Creative Commons license.

Anna Fox for Test Track; Darren Wittko for photos of Animal Kingdom Lodge, and Pirates of the Caribbean; Daryl Mitchell for Pop Century; Darryl Kenyon for Kali River Rapids; d.k.peterson (Flickr user) for Disney Princess Half Marathon; Mark & Paul Luukkonen for Princess Fairytale Hall, Canada Pavilion and The Barnstormer; 'Flickr mjurn' for Old Key West; Greg Goebel for Astro Orbiter; Harshlight (Flickr user) for photos of Mad Tea Party, Seven Dwarfs Mine Train and Peter Pan's Flight; Inzakira (Flickr user) for Living with the Land; Jeff Kays for Blizzard Beach, Buzz Lightyear Space Ranger Spin and Soarin; Joseph Brent for ESPN Wide World of Sports; Justin Ennis for Jungle Cruise; Kyosuke Takayama for Norway Pavilion; Leigh Caldwell for the Halloween Party photo; Lou Oms ci Imagination Pavilion; Luis Brizzante for Spaceship Earth; Matthew Freeman for Splash Mountain; Michael Gray for photos of Mickey's Philharmagic, Monster's Inc, Stitch's Great Escape, Caribbean Beach resort, EPCOT Food and Wine festival, and Holiday Splendor; Paul Hudson for Disney Springs and Mexico Pavilion; 'Paula and Cathy' for Turtle Talk; 'marada' for Cinderella Castle, in Fantasyland Section of guide; QuesterMark (Flickr user) for Contemporary Resort; Rhys A for Beach Club; rickpilot_2000 (Flickr user) for Typhoon Lagoon and Dinosaur; Sam Howzit for The Many Adventures of Winnie the Pooh, Very Merry Christmas Party, Big Thunder Mountain and it's a small world; Sonja - EPCOT Holidays around the World; Wikimedia for Primeval Whirl and Flower and Garden Festival; zannaland (Flickr user) for Sorcerer's of the Magic Kingdom and The Barnstomer; Big Front Page Image - Phillie Casablanca, Back Castle at night photo - Frank H Phillips; Sorcerers of the Magic Kingdom - zannaland; Tom Sawyer Island - Chad Sparkes; Philharmagic - Sam Howzit; Turtle Talk with Crush, Jedi Training, Triceratop Spin - Theme Park Tourist; Voyage of the Little Mermaid - Loren Javier; Walt Disney Presents, EPCOT Festival of the Arts - Harshlight; Indiana Jones - Thomas Jung; Gorilla - Corey Ann; "it all started with a mouse" - Disney Parks Blog; Up! A Great Bird Aventure - Joel (coconut wireless); Na'vi River Journey - mliu92; and Lego Store - mrice1996; Happily Ever After - Anthony Quintano

Printed in Great Britain
by Amazon